CW01312865

I Will Be Glad

Dr Richard Laugharne

What readers are saying.

In today's fast paced world people are swept forward in a tsunami of expectations and materialism. This is making people move away from the bigger unanswered questions in life such as 'Who are we', 'Why do we exist' and 'What is our purpose'? This absence of seeking an inner and deeper self has left humanity more forlorn and more likely to succumb to depression. Faith provides a safe harbour and anchor for us humans when the waves become dangerous and turbulent, particularly when it is a question of emotional anguish. This is the premise from which Dr Richard Laugharne has constructed his discourse, hinged on the two passions of his life: faith and mental health. He uses the words of God and the Church to provide a critical framework to understand depression. He addresses humanity's emotional suffering from a Biblical perspective to explore the cause and effect of the human predisposition to damaging beliefs and behaviours and the emotional distress we may experience as a result.
Dr Laugharne's book might well be the 'Noah's Ark' for the ongoing tsunami.
Professor Rohit Shankar FRCPsych MBE
Chair of Psychiatry, University of Plymouth

I Will Be Glad is refreshingly concise. In fluent language, Richard describes complex medical phenomena and marries them with clear theological principles in intriguing and fascinating ways. It is great to reflect on how God is good and full of grace in spite of the often painful and disturbing experiences of life and circumstances around us. I Will Be Glad offers deeply provoking, relevant and necessary reflections. Many people, like myself, can be rightly challenged and richly blessed through Richard's writing.
Dr Ben Basterfield: MRCP MRCGP
General Practioner

[I Will Be Glad is] …brilliant: practical, loving, honest and insightful.
Noëlle Molton : Consultant CGA Technologies

Depression of any kind is debilitating. Spiritual depression is particularly frightening for those of faith as it threatens to crush and dismantle their whole view of God and themselves. During forty-three years of ordained ministry, I have encountered many instances where a person is suffocated by guilt and a sense of inadequacy because they do not feel as they think (or are told) they should as a person of faith.

In this book, Richard Laugharne sets out common causes of depression and lifts the guilt. He is unambiguous about his faith and trust in God. He is hard-hitting over portrayals of the nature of God which pedal fear and guilt. He proclaims a God of deep compassion, yearning and love for every soul, revealed in Jesus Christ.

The Venerable John Reed, Archdeacon of Taunton 1999 – 2016.

This short book manages to be deeply practical, theologically rich and spiritually insightful at the same time. As an experienced psychiatrist, the author understands the complexities of being human, and how guilt, shame, anger and lust can lead to destructive behaviour towards ourselves and others. As a faithful follower of Jesus, he also knows about God's generous and grace-filled love, and how it can transform us. I recommend this book to anyone struggling with depression, anxiety or mental illness, to those who walk alongside them and to anyone who wants to know more about themselves and the God who created them and who loves them.

Rt Revd Hugh Nelson, Bishop of St Germans

Copyright Permissions

Scripture quotations taken from The Holy Bible, New International Version® NIV®
Copyright © 1973, 1978, 1984, 2011 by Biblica, Inc.
Used with permission. All rights reserved worldwide.

Scripture quotations marked MSG are taken from THE MESSAGE, copyright © 1993, 2002, 2018 by Eugene H. Peterson. Used by permission of NavPress. All rights reserved. Represented by Tyndale House Publishers, a Division of Tyndale House Ministries.

KJV: Scriptures marked KJV are taken from the KING JAMES VERSION (KJV): KING JAMES VERSION, public domain.

Dedication

In memory of Diana Laugharne, who read the early chapters of this book and encouraged me to continue.

Contents

Preface

Is following Jesus Christ good for your mental health? That is quite a complicated question. Jesus did not promise that it would be and did not suggest that was a good reason for following him. But he did say he would give us life in all its abundance and would ease our burden by giving us an easier yoke. He also said his followers would be despised and persecuted which can be a challenge to our mental wellbeing. Many Christians do suffer from depression and have struggled with confusion and even guilt for doing so. I believe a mature faith can combat spiritual causes of depression and ease the suffering for those who, sometimes for reasons no-one can understand, suffer from depression. I have worked as a psychiatrist in the British National Health Service for over 30 years and I am a lay minister in the Church of England, so these questions have always intrigued me. I have often pondered them sitting in the pew or the clinic when I should have been listening to someone else! The aim of this book is to consider how our beliefs about God impact on our emotional health. My underlying proposition is that if we get our theology wrong, our distorted faith can make us depressed. If we get our theology right, our faith will protect us from spiritual depression.

During the twentieth century many psychiatrists and psychologists expressed antipathy to religion. Eminent thinkers such as Sigmund Freud and Albert Ellis suggested that religious belief was a source of neurosis and that psychotherapies should discourage faith to promote better mental health (Moreira-Almeida et al., 2006). Freud, the father of psychoanalytical psychotherapy, wrote that religion results in 'depressing the value of life and distorting the picture of the real world in a delusional manner—which presupposes an intimidation of the intelligence' (Freud, 1962, p. 31). Other psychoanalysts, such as Jung and Guntrip were more accepting of the positive influence of faith. However, Ellis, an author of rational-emotive therapy, a precursor of cognitive-behavioural therapy, stated in 1980 that religiosity 'is in many respects equivalent to irrational thinking and emotional disturbance … the less religious (people) are the more emotionally healthy they will tend to be' (p. 637).

These assertions were based more on opinion than on evidence. In the last three decades empirical research has shown a very different picture (Koenig et al., 2012). A systematic review summarised the results of 147 independent studies on the association between religiousness and depression involving 98,975 subjects (Smith et al., 2003). The authors found that religiousness is modestly but robustly associated with lower levels of depressive symptoms. This finding did not vary for different ages, genders or ethnic groups. Another study discovered that the association between religiousness and fewer depressive symptoms is stronger for people under severe life stress, suggesting that the beneficial effect of faith is greater for people under pressure. Further research found that for those suffering from a depressive illness, religious motivation was associated with faster recovery (Koenig et al., 1998).

These papers suggest that faith can help people cope with severe stress and recover more quickly from depressive illnesses. It seems that Freud and Ellis were wrong. This raises further questions. Why is religious faith helpful when depressed? Which aspects of religious faith protect people from developing depression? This book will not attempt to answer these questions exhaustively, but it is important to take hold of the hope we have in our faith and be encouraged that there is strong evidence that our faith can build us up.

In 1965, Dr Martyn Lloyd-Jones, a renowned pastor and preacher of the twentieth century who was also a medical doctor, published a series of sermons he had delivered at Westminster Chapel in London entitled *Spiritual Depression.* It is still in print and has sold many copies over the last 50 years. I read *Spiritual Depression* as a Christian and psychiatrist and was struck by how important it was and still is. I wanted both to point people towards the book and to contribute to the discussion as a psychiatrist and as a person trying to follow Christ at the beginning of the twenty-first century. I cannot compete with the pastoral experience or theological depth of knowledge of Lloyd-Jones. I can bring some insight as a psychiatrist with 30 years' experience of talking to people suffering from depression and add to his important insights into God's revelation of the human condition for a contemporary readership; I can also introduce insights from wise authors published since 1965. I have therefore recast some of his important messages and introduced some of my own thoughts on the subject.

I hope they prove helpful.

Reflection

I started this book at a time when my wife had a recurrence of cancer in 2009. Seven years later she died. She read the early chapters and encouraged me to continue writing. We were aware of how precious and temporary this life is and we had some great times over those seven years as she had long periods of wellness and abundance. We also had times of great anxiety and sadness. A really difficult time was in the last five months, but even then, there were significant moments, precious to both of us and of lasting importance for me. Looking back, writing these chapters was one of my ways of coping. Offering them on to an audience now is a recognition of the value these thoughts still have for me and may have for others.

Chapter 1

Understanding spiritual depression.

As the deer pants for streams of water,
so my soul pants for you, my God.
2 My soul thirsts for God, for the living God.
When can I go and meet with God?
3 My tears have been my food
day and night,
while people say to me all day long,
'Where is your God?'
4 These things I remember
as I pour out my soul:
how I used to go to the house of God
under the protection of the Mighty One
with shouts of joy and praise
among the festive throng.

5 Why, my soul, are you downcast?
Why so disturbed within me?
Put your hope in God,
for I will yet praise him,
my Saviour and my God.

6 My soul is downcast within me;
therefore I will remember you
from the land of the Jordan,
the heights of Hermon – from Mount Mizar.
7 Deep calls to deep
in the roar of your waterfalls;
all your waves and breakers
have swept over me.

8 By day the LORD directs his love,
at night his song is with me –
a prayer to the God of my life.

9 I say to God my Rock,
'Why have you forgotten me?
Why must I go about mourning,
oppressed by the enemy?'
10 My bones suffer mortal agony
as my foes taunt me,
saying to me all day long,
'Where is your God?'

[11] Why, my soul, are you downcast?
Why so disturbed within me?
Put your hope in God,
for I will yet praise him,
my Saviour and my God.
(Psalm 42, NIV).

The book of psalms is, like the Bible as a whole, an honest book. It does not present us with an idealised view of life where everything is straightforward and makes sense. It is beautiful and messy, with a range of human reactions to the difficult situations we find ourselves in, some of our own making, some not. Psalms 42 and 43 reflect a person who is spiritually depressed. They are downcast, tearful, struggling to sleep, ruminating on the past and struggling to find hope for the future.

I believe everyone who has a faith (if they live long enough) will struggle with spiritual depression at some point and this is reflected in the experience of many significant characters in the Bible. But before we look at this it would be worth reflecting on what we might mean by spiritual depression.

Severe depression and less severe depression

As a psychiatrist I would distinguish between severe depression and mild to moderate depression. Severe depression has physical and psychological symptoms or characteristics and can also lead to psychotic symptoms when very severe. The core psychological symptoms can be a loss of interest in life, a loss of enjoyment in the things we normally enjoy and low mood. They can also include feelings of guilt, worthlessness, hopelessness and despair about the future.

The physical symptoms of severe depression include poor sleep, especially waking early in the morning, loss of appetite and weight (although the opposites can also occur), low energy, poor concentration, feeling worse in the mornings and a general slowing in our thought and activities.

When severe, symptoms labelled as psychosis can occur in depression. Delusions are fixed, false beliefs held firmly against any evidence and not in keeping with the person's social, educational or cultural background. Psychosis also includes hallucinations which are false sensory perceptions, most commonly hearing voices. The delusions 'fit the mood' of the depression, so can be ideas of persecution, guilt, impending death or that parts of the body are not functioning. They often reflect the persons underlying belief system, so for someone of faith they may be of abandonment by God, persecution by the devil or a concrete, bizarre religious belief. They are delusional if they are bizarre according to the person's usual beliefs and the beliefs of their spiritual peers. Hallucinations in severe depression are usually voices talking to the sufferer, again fitting the mood. They are often accusatory, telling the patient that they are without hope and sometimes telling them to kill themselves. The bleakness of Psalm 88 suggests some of the sense of abandonment by God that can be felt when people of faith experience severe depression. Suicidal feelings are remarkably common in society, but in severe depression can be more intense. When risks are higher, people can make suicidal plans and attempts.

Reflection

An example of someone of faith suffering from severe depression might be Robert. Robert is in a position of leadership in his local church and has been made redundant from his job due to staff cutbacks in the company. He feels a failure and is worried about how he can pay the bills, especially as his children are teenagers and are getting involved in many activities in and outside of school. He begins to get irritable with his family and spends more time in bed and on his own. He begins to tell his wife that people at church are talking about him and think he should not be a worship leader, even though she has seen no evidence of this. He stops going to church or attending meetings, and the pastor expresses concern to his wife because he is not answering emails. When the pastor finally gets to see him, Robert says he feels abandoned by God and convinced he is going to hell. When the pastor asks why, he discloses he is hearing a voice at night saying things like, 'You are useless, you cannot keep a job and everyone knows you should not be leading anything' and, 'You may as well get on with it, everyone would be better off without you'.

Robert is persuaded to visit his GP and agrees to see the local mental health team. He starts medication and is visited regularly by a psychiatric nurse. Over several weeks he begins to feel a little better and is willing to see friends again. Gradually his confidence returns and the voices fade and disappear. After a few months, with the help of an occupational therapist, he finds a new job. Six months later he is back to his normal self and able to tell his story to others who are going through similar experiences. His wife says he is more empathetic with others who struggle with their mental health.

When someone has severe depression, especially when they have psychotic symptoms, they cannot be reasoned with and attempts to do so can be frustrating for the carer as well as the patient. I have treated many people with severe depression and they usually need medical help, often with medication, before they are accessible for talking treatments or counselling. Rarely non-invasive brain stimulation, or neuromodulation treatments, such as electroconvulsive therapy, vagal nerve stimulation[1] or transcranial magnetic stimulation can be needed and effective. This book is not primarily to help those suffering from this severe depression but it is important to have some understanding of depression that presents with psychotic symptoms.

[1] The vagal nerves carry signals from the digestive system, heart and other organs to the brain and back again. Stimulating a vagal nerve can signal to your body that it's time to relax and de-stress. Long-term improvements in mood, wellbeing and resilience can result, and this treatment also can help reduce epileptic seizures.

By the term spiritual depression, I refer to people of faith whose spiritual beliefs play a prominent part in their worldview: who are suffering from a depressive illness and therefore the understanding of how to overcome their difficulties incorporates a strong spiritual dimension. Spiritual depression is more likely to be mild to moderate in intensity. They may have some of the psychological symptoms listed above and suicidal feelings can occur. The physical features can be evident but the psychotic symptoms of severe depression are less likely. Fundamentally, we can be reasoned with when not severely depressed and so talking therapies are used in the clinical world, such as cognitive behavioural therapy, psychodynamic psychotherapy and many other schools of talking treatments. For people of faith, having someone to talk to, who understands their beliefs, may be important to them, and they will often speak to their pastor, priest or a friend they trust. I think this is a healthy role for people in the church and many have experience in giving such help.

Spiritual depression in the Bible

There are many examples of spiritual depression in the Bible. Elijah, after his remarkable and miraculous victory over the priests of Baal, gets the message from Jezebel that she will kill him. He flees into the desert and sits down, wanting to die. He has had enough: more than he feels he can take. He wants it all to stop and is suicidal. Interestingly God sends an angel who does not get into a spiritual discussion with him. The angel brings him food and tells him to get a good night's sleep. Good advice. Then, when he is feeling physically better, God meets with him to talk things over and come up with a plan. It is significant that Elijah hits rock bottom after a great spiritual achievement.

Reflection

It is not uncommon to read of church leaders who hit a dark patch when they are at the height of so-called success in their careers. Rob Bell has written of his experience of this phenomenon when he was pastoring a mega-church as has John Mark Comer, the author of The Ruthless Elimination of Hurry.

Job is the opposite. He gets depressed and suicidal after catastrophic life events that would certainly have a similar effect on most of us. We have no problem in understanding his depression. His reaction and his well-meaning friends' impulsively offered advice have furnished a most powerful meditation on spiritual depression over the centuries. His situation is aggravated by their interventions - a cautionary tale for those of us who do not reflect enough before we speak.

Saul's is a disturbing story of a man who makes bad decisions from his position of power, abuses his authority and becomes depressed: tormented by his negative thoughts and increasingly paranoid about the motives of others, he becomes a risk to those around him. He believes David is plotting to overthrow him because of his popularity with the people. His depression appears to spill over into psychosis, and his story is a lesson to all those who exercise power.

Reflection

We have seen similar bizarre behaviour from our politicians who strive for years to get to the top but who, when they get there, become obsessed with those who might be rivals. This led Richard Nixon, President of the United States (1969-1974), to break the law and so be removed from office in disgrace. In the UK, Tony Blair and Gordon Brown, despite winning three general elections and being the two most powerful people in the country, allowed their intense rivalry and suspicion of each other to ruin their relationship and affect the functioning of the whole government.

Moses also seems to get depressed but often from exasperation at the behaviour of those he leads and the burden of leadership. He is constantly being criticised for any difficulties and the stress affects his behaviour.

David appears to experience spiritual depression on a regular basis, initially under the pressure of being a persecuted outlaw. Later he becomes complacent in his comfortable kingship. He commits adultery with Bathsheba and engineers the death of her husband to cover up their affair. As a result of the murder of Uriah, his family breaks down. His son leads a rebellion against him and is killed, but David, knowing that the family chaos is partly of his own making, is overwhelmed with grief. His story demonstrates that a remarkably spiritual man can make big mistakes. His had lifelong consequences which he had to live with.

John the Baptiser was someone whom we will examine in a later chapter, but we will note here that after his imprisonment, he doubted whether he was right in identifying Jesus as the Messiah. I suspect that in his prison cell he started to question his judgement and despair at his situation.

Even Jesus Christ suffered entirely understandable acute anxiety when he was in the Garden of Gethsemane. This would not be an anxiety illness under modern medical parlance as it is an appropriate reaction to the extreme stress he was feeling as he contemplated his imminent painful death. Nevertheless, the symptoms were similar, with fear, insomnia and extreme sweating.

What can we learn about spiritual depression from the Bible? Well, firstly we can take lessons from the accounts of these peoples' lives. The lessons we learn will not be exhaustive but have the potential to enlighten our own experiences. Secondly, from the non-narrative books of the Bible we can learn from direct teaching, such as that contained in the Pentateuch, the wisdom books in the Old Testament, the parables of Christ and the epistles of the New Testament. There is wisdom from God in this teaching on how we may prevent, and how we may deal with, spiritual depression.

The causes of spiritual depression

Martin Lloyd-Jones (1998 p.12) lists what he believed were possible causes of spiritual depression and his account bears up fifty years later.

1. Temperament:
    a. Know yourself: Our temperament or personality is determined by several things, including characteristics we inherit from our parents, our upbringing and events in our childhood. We used to call this nature and nurture but now we talk of the interaction between genes and our environment. What is important is that we reflect and get to know ourselves: how we tick, the strengths and weaknesses of our personality. Some of us are

more prone to depression, introspection and melancholy than others, and understanding this is important in dealing with our emotional responses to life's events.

Reflection

Personally, I am prone to being morbidly inward looking and self-preoccupied and concerned how others view me. This can make me a little paranoid, in the common use of the term not the psychiatric condition of persecutory delusions. But I am not as vulnerable to anxiety as others and generally not a worrier. When reacting to situations I try to remember these tendencies and not overreact accordingly.

b. Our strengths can make us vulnerable as much as our weaknesses. When we have certain strengths, we can use these qualities in a damaging way. An obvious example is people who have charismatic personalities which can engage people in great causes but can lead them into adulterous relationships undermining their good work. Highly intelligent people can believe their own opinions are so sophisticated they stop even considering that they might be wrong and their over-confidence can lead to profound mistakes.

   c. Introspection: Whilst self-examination can lead to better functioning, morbid introspection can lead to spiritual depression and self-absorption.

2. Physical illness: It should not be forgotten that many physical illnesses can present themselves as, or lead to, depression. If we are depressed and cannot understand why, it is important to get checked for common physical illnesses such as hypothyroidism or diabetes. It can be a mistake to look for spiritual answers to everything. Our Christian faith is a holistic faith, and our bodies can affect our spiritual functioning and vice versa. Also remember that many medications can have the side effect of lowering mood.
3. A reaction to events: these can be good and bad events or changes in our lives. Job is the obvious example of a reaction to bad events, as is David after the complicated

bereavement of his rebellious son, Absalom. Elijah, on the other hand, reacts to the massive 'come-down' of his triumph on Mount Carmel which might, for a different person, have been a tremendous confidence-builder.

4. Spiritual attack: an overlap, perhaps, with the 'come-down' phenomenon described above, but we have an adversary who wants us to function badly spiritually, to be depressed and downhearted. After times of spiritual significance and effective service, we may be especially vulnerable to spiritual attacks designed to keep us from God.
5. Bad theology: this is really the subject of this whole book. I believe a significant source of spiritual depression comes from false understandings of God, distorted ideas about ourselves and dysfunctional relationships with others that can be improved if we wrestle with the Bible for a better understanding on how we can relate to God, ourselves and each other.

The following chapters address some issues in the theological understanding of how we relate to God, ourselves and others. I believe theological reflection on these relationships not only informs how we understand our psychological functioning but can also protect us from spiritual depression. That does not mean we will not have times of sadness but we can enter into life in all its abundance. It does not mean we will not need to wrestle with God- the very name of Israel means ‘wrestling with God’. Wrestling with God is one of the reasons I go to church!

Chapter 2

Understanding the grace and goodness of God: combating a pagan view of God.

The serpent was clever, more clever than any wild animal GOD had made. He spoke to the Woman: 'Do I understand that God told you not to eat from any tree in the garden?'

2-3 The Woman said to the serpent, 'Not at all. We can eat from the trees in the garden. It's only about the tree in the middle of the garden that God said, "Don't eat from it; don't even touch it or you'll die."'

4-5 The serpent told the Woman, 'You won't die. God knows that the moment you eat from that tree, you'll see what's really going on. You'll be just like God, knowing everything, ranging all the way from good to evil.'

6 When the Woman saw that the tree looked like good eating and realised what she would get out of it—she'd know everything!—she took and ate the fruit and then gave some to her husband, and he ate.

7 Immediately the two of them did 'see what's really going on'—saw themselves naked! They sewed fig leaves together as makeshift clothes for themselves.

8 When they heard the sound of GOD strolling in the garden in the evening breeze, the Man and his Wife hid in the trees of the garden, hid from GOD.

Genesis 3: 1-8 (MSG)

'It is much worse to have a false idea of God than no idea at all'

William Temple[2]

---

[2] Widely attributed

There is a book of sermons on the first ten chapters of Genesis by the theologian Helmut Thielke entitled *How the World Began.* He observes that the serpent distorts Eve's very view of God when he is tempting her to eat the forbidden fruit. The serpent does not argue about God's existence, he argues that her view, that God is good, is wrong. He says that God is not telling the truth: that the fruit is forbidden not because human beings will die if they eat it, but because God does not want rivals, and does not want the best for them. God is not trustworthy. He wants to keep them in their place. He is not good. This crucial insight cannot be emphasised enough. A great source of spiritual depression is a false idea of God - that he is not good but bad: that he is angry and wants to harm us. Many Christians would struggle to acknowledge this openly and consciously but carry this subconsciously or unconsciously and our culture can encourage this view of the Christian God as 'not good'. Vocal atheists like Dawkins, Hitchens and Harris state that the God of the Bible is sadistic and vindictive or impotent or simply a myth and award-winning authors like Pullman and McEwan drive similar narratives in their compelling works of fiction.

These perspectives do not arise out of nothing.

The issue of suffering challenges all of us to ask why terrible things happen to innocent people - a question that is articulated by many Christian authors and is expressed repeatedly in scripture: in the Psalms most passionately. C.S.Lewis, addressing these issues in his books *The Problem of Pain* and *God in the Dock*, identified the tendency for modern humanity to accuse God of being to blame for injustice in the world rather than examining humankind's tendency to sinfulness. I remember talking to an atheist friend about faith and he said to me, 'I don't believe in God, but if he does exist, he's a bastard'.

The image of nature as 'red in tooth and claw' (Tennyson, 1891) also challenges our attribution of goodness to God as creator. The natural world seems to depend on predation, violence and death. Evidence from palaeontology and other sciences suggests that this pre-dates the coming of human beings and questions the theocracy (the justice) of God (Southgate, 2002). Many Christians have asserted that evil entered creation when Adam and Eve first sinned, but the evil committed and provoked by the serpent occurs before any rebellion by human beings. The spiritual battle is already joined before humans enter the fray.

This scripture from the book of Genesis gives us insight into how one fundamental front in this battle is the attack on our minds: to distort our view of God, and this, I believe, is a significant source of spiritual depression. It prevents people from turning to God and undermines the faith of those who have done so. Indeed, the teachings, death and resurrection of Jesus Christ are precisely the means by which God is redressing this distortion – because they reveal the true nature and character of God.

Reverting to a pagan view of God

We so frequently return to a view of God that is pagan - a God who is angry, who resents our autonomy and whom we need to appease. This has been articulated very well by Rob Bell in his DVD *The Gods Aren't Angry*. For a pagan God, what we do is never enough. God is angry that we fail to be perfect, and bad things that happen to us are a judgement from him.

Reflection

One friend I have is a great befriender and often invites people to church who have very little experience of going or have never been. A frequent response is, 'I couldn't possibly go to church, I might be struck down by lightening!' Jokes often reveal how we think.

A former neighbour of mine was a dentist. He had a comfortable life, but suddenly developed an arthritic illness affecting his hands which is pretty devastating for a dentist. I remember meeting him at the school gates and talking about this situation, and he suddenly said, 'What have I done to deserve this?'

This is an idea I frequently hear stated, by friends as well as patients: a primeval belief that we are subject to the anger of an insecure God who does not want the best for us and is eager to punish us for our faults. It is also evident that there is a human instinct to believe that the misfortunes of others are self-inflicted through moral or other shortcomings.

In the book of Job, his friends insist that his disasters are self-inflicted due to his undiscovered sins, which he adamantly denies, and we know is not true from the first chapters. God vindicates Job and chastises his friends. In the gospels, the disciples asked, 'If someone is born disabled, is it the result of their sin or their parents' sin?' They still had a view of a punishing God. Jesus gives an emphatic, 'No, this is not right', whilst, as in the book of Job, not giving an easy explanation.

Reflection

When my wife was ill with cancer, she noticed that, whenever someone was diagnosed, people would try to give an explanation: They ate the wrong food, did not do enough exercise, lived too near a mobile telephone mast. (There is no evidence for phone masts causing cancer). They could not accept that sometimes we do not have a reason, an explanation, why bad things happen, just as Job received no explanation. People tend to want to blame the person or someone else. There must be a judgement somewhere.

Christians are also subject to these distorted beliefs. They try to be good, but are never good enough. They pray, but feel they never pray enough. They believe, but they don't believe enough. They serve in their church, but don't serve enough. They give money, but do not give enough. Sometimes church authorities and pastors can use this distorted theology manipulatively to impose guilt on their congregations and can even preach that people are not healthy or wealthy because of their spiritual failures. This can be a source of spiritual abuse.

This is a distorted Christianity which thinks about God as someone to be appeased. This thinking is oppressive and there is an overlap here with cognitive theories of depression, in which distorted thinking patterns can lead to depression. If we believe in the love of God and the grace of God, we need to think differently to this.

Reflection

I know of a committed Christian family who experienced the tragic death of a child in a road accident. After this terrible event, the father was contacted by fellow Christians who suggested to him that the only explanation for what had happened was that he must have committed adultery. He had not. This theology is strikingly unbiblical and potentially so devastating to those suffering terribly already. The idea that if something bad has happened to someone of faith, they must be being punished for a sin is deeply unbiblical and deeply pagan. Likewise, if life is going very well, this does not mean God thinks more highly of you than others, but we can be thankful for the blessings God gives us.

At the heart of the universe is perfect harmony and no dissonance. God is good and loves us unconditionally. He wants our company and wants to forgive us all we get wrong. To really believe this is difficult because our human experience of love is so often conditional. But to glimpse this truth is to be transformed.

We have some notable examples of this transformation in our understanding of God in Christian history. Martin Luther was a devoted monk who put his devotion into practice, but this consecrated life was oppressive rather than liberating. He, perhaps, was an example of a man who prayed but never felt he prayed enough. His view of God was transformed on studying the epistle to the Romans. John Wesley was also an earnest Christian minister who dedicated his life to God but felt excluded from God's salvation. It was during a sermon at Aldersgate in London, again on Romans when his heart 'was strangely warmed'[3], that he realised that he did not have to earn God's love but that it was a gift of grace, through faith. This changed his life! He was already a follower of Christ but had not understood the nature of God and his salvation - an understanding that transformed his life and ministry.

If Luther and Wesley could have a distorted view of God, it is not surprising that many Christians (perhaps all of us at some time) can slip back into a pagan understanding of God. Perhaps it is another of Satan's great lies, along with a distorted view of God, that we have to earn our own salvation. One of the great tragedies of modern Western culture is that it views Christianity as an oppressive story restricting peoples' lives. But the truth is that God sent Christ to die for us before we acted or asked. The act of our salvation is finished and completed. It is a gift of grace which we only have to accept. This is so hard to believe, it is such good news, and it is such a wonderful understanding of God. Any activity from us has no

---

[3] John Wesley's Journal: Wednesday May 24th, 1738.

relevance to our salvation. Ideally (and we struggle to reach any ideal) our faith is only a response to the love of God.

Sometimes Christians struggle to accept this salvation (especially for those we regard as rather unacceptable) and can become like the Pharisees in the gospels. Jesus warned us against a religious resentment at the forgiving love of God. (We shall look at this in chapter 4.) God does not need to be appeased. As St Augustine of Hippo summed up so well, 'Love God and do what you want'[4]. Augustine has sometimes been accused of having a bleak view of human beings with his emphasis on original sin, but the flip side to this coin is a wonderful, and accurate, view of a loving, forgiving God who will do everything for us rather than demand that we do anything for him. And it is the way of this grace, the death and resurrection of Christ, that ultimately demonstrates the goodness of God. He enters the world to share in our suffering and is not aloof from it. We do not understand why some suffer so much, but we know that God suffers with us. This is the evidence of his goodness.

---

[4] Augustine of Hippo, Seventh Homily on 1 John 4:4-12.

Therefore, we need to constantly be vigilant in how we understand God. We must be vigilant that our view of God is not determined by our own lives, neither the good nor the bad life-events. We need to remind ourselves that God is good and God is love. His love is unconditional, for all people, and no-one is outside that love, including those people we find most unlovable. And meditating on the true nature of God will make us glad and protect us from depression.

Chapter 3

Understanding the invisibility of God: combating the pursuit of our own significance.

Be careful not to practise your righteousness in front of others to be seen by them. If you do, you will have no reward from your Father in heaven.
So, when you give to the needy, do not announce it with trumpets, as the hypocrites do in the synagogues and on the streets, to be honoured by others. Truly I tell you, they have received their reward in full. But when you give to the needy, do not let your left hand know what your right hand is doing, so that your giving may be in
secret. Then your Father, who sees what is done in secret, will reward you.
And when you pray, do not be like the hypocrites, for they love to pray standing in the synagogues and on the street corners to be seen by others. Truly I tell you, they have received their reward in full. But when you pray, go into your room, close the door and pray to your Father, who is unseen. Then your Father, who sees what is done in secret, will reward you.

When you fast, do not look sombre as the hypocrites do, for they disfigure their faces to show others they are fasting. Truly I tell you, they have received their reward in full. But when you fast, put oil on your head and wash your face, so that it will not be obvious to others that you are fasting, but only to your Father, who is unseen; and your Father, who sees what is done in secret, will reward you.

(Matthew 6: 1-6, 16-18 NIV)

Now to the King eternal, immortal, invisible, the only God, be honour and glory.

(1 Tim 1:17 NIV)

We can often be painfully aware of the invisibility of God, especially when life is difficult. Why is God so invisible? Why does God make it difficult to hear him, believe in him, and feel his presence? If he is omnipotent, omnipresent and omniscient, this seems a strange way to show it. Why, in this world which needs his love and presence so much, does he feel so inaccessible to so many? Phillip Yancey, in his book *Disappointment with God*, identifies three common internal questions posed by people struggling with faith: is God fair? why is God silent? and why is God hidden?

But to turn the coin around, what does this say about the nature of God, and if we are to seek to be like God, to follow his example, how should we lead our lives?

God does not force his presence on us. He seems to be content to be in the background, to the extent that many simply do not believe in his existence. To find him, we often need to actively seek him. He seems strangely willing to be ignored. At times he seems an elusive character. The one time a human being asks Him what his name is, He gives the most evasive answer in history: YHWH, I will be what I will be, I am who I am, or is it the sound of breathing, and we whisper God's name every time we exhale (Bell, 2006). When he speaks to Elijah, after the earth, wind and fire, it is in a whisper. When he appears to Moses, the prophet sees just the back of his head. Indeed, the scriptures say no-one has seen this God who spoke the universe into existence.

Jesus, whom we believe to be God as human being, also, in his life here, seemed frequently, although not always, to go out of His way to avoid attention. He would travel from place to place, moving on when attention grew too great. When he healed people, he sent them home to avoid the village or asked them not to speak of it. When he did have crowds following him, he lost them by delivering teaching that was difficult to understand, ending up with a small group of disciples who fled when the final trouble started. He was aware that 'going public' in Jerusalem would lead to his abandonment and death.

I was preparing a sermon on Thomas and found only three references to Thomas in the gospels. However, this is quite a few considering the invisibility of personal references to the twelve disciples. Peter gets quite a few, James and John, hardly any, but most of the others have no personal mention at all. Judas, unfortunately, is known more than the others but for all the wrong reasons. When the disciples do come into the gospel story, it is often far from flattering. These eleven men, after Judas' death, changed the world more than any group in history, but, to us, most of them are invisible.

A striking thing about Christian history is that when the church becomes powerful it often goes wrong. Imposing Christian values appears to lead to oppression and abuse. When Christians are strident and insistent that their opinion dominates, bad things seem to happen. Theocracy never seems to work in this world, as flawed human beings claim the authority of God for their own desires.

Reflection

It also seems that Christian fame or celebrity can lead to great difficulties. Many famous Christian leaders are embroiled in scandal. In recent years two revered Christians, one from a Catholic tradition, Jean Vanier, and another from the evangelical tradition, Ravi Zacharias, have been exposed, after they have died, as men who abused people sexually, leaving many disillusioned. It seems fame can lead to pride, temptation, a sense of entitlement and the exploitation of others.

On the other hand, one of the most significant episodes of church growth in history has occurred in the last 50 years in China. The church there is persecuted and so the growth has been in small groups quietly meeting in peoples' homes. Of necessity, we know of no famous names amongst these Chinese Christians. It is now estimated that there are 100 million Christians in China, more than the number of members of the Chinese communist party, and possibly more than in any other nation on earth. This is a quiet movement of God, largely unnoticed by the rest of the world.

Egoism and humility

Jesus Christ was humble. As described in the famous passage in Philippians, he was willing to empty himself of his deity and become a human being, to serve others and to suffer and die a humiliating and painful death. I remember going to Jerusalem and walking to one possible site of the crucifixion outside the Damascus gate, where the cliff still has the shape of a skull. At the base of the cliff was a dirty, busy bus station. How entirely appropriate, as when Jesus was crucified people were just walking past, hurling sarcastic insults at him or ignoring him entirely. This was a man who was not thinking of his ego.

We are called to be like this. However, we can get caught up in our own ego. Richard Rohr in his book *The World, the Flesh and the Devil,* observes that when Paul writes of 'the flesh' in his epistles, a closer modern translation would be the ego. It is a focus on our own selves.

As Christians we are often keen to be noticed. We desire recognition and significance. To be anonymous is difficult for our egos. We are anxious that we will not be remembered when we die. On a more collective level, we seem to believe that the Church needs to be vocal, strident in making its views heard. We seem to think God calls us to speak for him and if we do not, he will be angry with us.

Is the way of following God to be invisible unless we are sought? To be active whilst not being noticed? To be willing to blend into the background whilst being the source of goodness? To be unremembered whilst being maximally effective? To never use power to put into practice the message but only the persuasion of our lives? Yancey (1988) observes that the God of the Bible does not desire above all things our obedience; He longs for our love, and that can only be given if we choose to give it as an act of free will - which also means we can choose not to. Maybe we are called to do his will and be quiet in the world, to let people come to us before we speak out. Many will not come, but that is their choice. We should invite them, but not forcefully.

Should we whisper rather than shout?

This, some might argue, goes against another of Jesus' teachings in the sermon on the mount in Matthew:

'You are the light of the world. A town built on a hill cannot be hidden. Neither do people light a lamp and put it under a bowl. Instead, they put it on its stand, and it gives light to everyone in the house. In the same way, let your light shine before others, that they may see your good deeds and glorify your Father in heaven.'

(Matthew 5:14-16)

But I do not think it does. Our light is the quality of our lives, individually and collectively, and does not reside in the stridency of our voices.

What has this got to do with spiritual depression? Elijah became depressed because he felt he was the only person left with faith in the true God, that his witness and example were ineffective and his dramatic acts ignored. In fact, he was not, there were seven thousand believers who had not turned to Baal. We can feel isolated in our faith and in despair at the indifference and unbelief of those around us. But we need to have faith in the true invisible God and his quiet ways of doing things, and not resort to desperate shouting. An idolatry of our recognition and our significance, like all idolatries, leads to disappointment, frustration and spiritual depression. Following the true God who is willing to be invisible, ignored and not believed is the path to true contentment.

Chapter 4

Understanding ourselves: combating spiritual narcissism, doubt and disappointment.

After this conversation, Jesus went on with his disciples into the Judean countryside and relaxed with them there. He was also baptising. At the same time, John was baptising over at Aenon near Salim, where water was abundant. This was before John was thrown into jail. John's disciples got into an argument with the establishment Jews over the nature of baptism. They came to John and said, 'Rabbi, you know the one who was with you on the other side of the Jordan? The one you authorised with your witness? Well, he's now competing with us. He's baptising, too, and everyone's going to him instead of us.'

John answered, 'It's not possible for a person to succeed—I'm talking about *eternal* success—without heaven's help. You yourselves were there when I made it public that I was not the Messiah but simply the one sent ahead of him to get things ready. The one who gets the bride is, by definition, the bridegroom. And the bridegroom's friend, his "best man"—that's me—in place at his side where he can hear every word, is genuinely happy. How could he be jealous when he knows that the wedding is finished and the marriage is off to a good start?

That's why my cup is running over. This is the assigned moment for him to move into the centre, while I slip off to the side-lines.'

(John 3: 22-31 MSG)

John's disciples reported back to him the news of all these events taking place. He sent two of them to the Master to ask the question, 'Are you the One we've been expecting, or are we still waiting?'

The men showed up before Jesus and said, 'John the Baptiser sent us to ask you, "Are you the One we've been expecting, or are we still waiting?"'

In the next two or three hours Jesus healed many from diseases, distress, and evil spirits. To many of the blind he gave the gift of sight. Then he gave his answer: 'Go back and tell John what you have just seen and heard:

The blind see,
The lame walk,
Lepers are cleansed,
The deaf hear,
The dead are raised,
The wretched of the earth
have God's salvation hospitality extended to them.

"Is this what you were expecting? Then count yourselves fortunate!'

After John's messengers left to make their report, Jesus said more about John to the crowd of people. 'What did you expect when you went to see him in the wild? A week-end camper? Hardly. What then? A sheik in silk pyjamas? Not in the wilderness, not by a long shot. What then? A messenger from God? That's right, a messenger! Probably the greatest messenger you'll even hear. He is the messenger Malachi announced when he wrote,

I'm sending my messenger on ahead
To make the road smooth for you.

Let me lay it out for you as plainly as I can: No-one in history surpasses John the Baptiser, but in the kingdom he prepared for you, the lowliest person is ahead of him.'

(Luke 7: 18-30, MSG)

John the Baptiser was a remarkable man. Yet his death was so awful, so meaningless, and so pathetic. He was imprisoned by Herod because he had criticised Herod's relationship with his brother's wife. Yet Herod liked to talk to him and listen to him. John was clearly a charismatic and inspiring speaker.

Herod, like many middle-aged men before and since, has his head turned by a younger woman. Drunk and with friends, he promises this woman anything. He falls into a trap, and she asks for the head of John. Herod, even if it is with reluctance and guilt, puts his reputation before John's life and has him killed. Are there any deaths in the scriptures more desperately futile? John was only a young man, and his ministry may have lasted less than a year. It seems such a waste - and yet describing John's life as a waste could not be further from the truth.

The striking thing about John's life is the seeming decline in his fortunes, yet his place in the divine plan could hardly be greater. His conception is celebrated almost as much as that of Christ himself. The poem of celebration of his birth by his father is still celebrated at the Morning Prayer service in the Church of England as the Benedictus. He was conceived through the will of God, with an angelic visitation to boot.

He then becomes a truly charismatic rabbi - and people flock to the desert to hear him and follow him. He is the first to declare the coming of the Messiah, and then to recognise who that Messiah is - his younger cousin from Nazareth. And that Man from Nazareth chooses to be baptised by John himself.

At this point John's disciples - for, as any first century rabbi, he has devoted followers - start to leave him: Andrew was one of these. Others say to John, 'Doesn't it bother you that your disciples are jumping ship and following this Jesus'. And his response is an example to us all, an attitude that will protect us from spiritual narcissism: that's OK, because 'He must increase, I must decrease' (that's the NIV translation).

But before we look at that response, the story of John does not then jump to his death. There is an episode that might represent John's lowest point, maybe a time of significant spiritual depression for him. After he has been imprisoned, he sends a message through his followers to Jesus. Are you really the Messiah, or should we be expecting someone else?

What? You are the man who first recognised Jesus for who he is, called him the Lamb of God: you baptised him! Didn't you see the Spirit coming down on him? Didn't you hear that voice from heaven? How can you of all people doubt him now?

Well, if we were stuck in a dungeon, facing a possible imminent death with brutal enemies in high places, we would, in all likelihood, have similar doubts. In fact, most of us will have similar doubts in far less desperate situations but in circumstances that challenge our faith and shake us to our very foundations. The fact that it happened to such a great man as John gives me solace. Jesus did not condemn him but reassured him with messianic observations straight from the Old Testament which John would have understood. I hope that John was reassured. We are not told how he responded. The Bible does not always tell us everything - it leaves us wondering. What we know is that John was killed soon afterwards. He never saw the fulfilment of Jesus' messianic mission. He never knew of the death and resurrection of his cousin, how God brought a new era, a new covenant to the people of the world, a new hope no-one had yet begun to imagine.

I believe we can learn much from this man.

i) Humility rather than spiritual narcissism: 'I must decrease, he must increase'. We are living in an era of an idolatry of the self, and Christians can be polluted by this spirit. We can become engrossed with our role in the Kingdom of God. A lay definition of narcissism can be self-preoccupation (Holmes, 2001), and I would describe spiritual narcissism as a preoccupation with our individual spiritual life. We can be self-obsessed with our significance in God's plans, and demand from others recognition of our vision for ourselves. Being ambitious for God can be a good thing, but we can become neurotically preoccupied with the question, 'What does God want from me?' This can be a source of great angst and lead to a spiritual depression because we have a paralysing preoccupation with our role in the Kingdom. We can become convinced if we do not 'hear' this from God we will take a wrong path and mess our lives up.

Reflection

I remember a time in my own life, a very exciting time, when I was involved in an alternative worship church in the early 1990s. We organised church services to resemble club culture, with dance music and projected images. We were very influenced by John Wimber and the Vineyard church with their emphasis on signs and wonders. But at the back of my mind, I always wanted an exciting prophecy about me, my future, my importance in the Kingdom of God, and when I did not get it, I was disappointed and envious of those who did. There were many good things from this period in my life, but I realised I was becoming narcissistic in my spiritual desires. It was hard to put the communal life of the whole group before my individual desires.

Narcissism is fundamentally lonely. We all too easily fail to follow John's example of being unconcerned with our own role in God's plans as long as Christ is at the centre and is glorified. If we do follow John's example, we can relax because we are not putting ourselves at the centre of our universe. This is truly liberating as the tyranny of self-absorption is dethroned in our lives. This release can give us a simple joy in our part in the story of the Kingdom of Heaven, knowing that however small that part is, it is of eternal significance to God. Benjamin Jowett, a Victorian theologian and Master at Balliol College, Oxford, is quoted by Henry Kissinger as saying we achieve a lot more if we don't care who gets the credit.[5]

Reflection

I have a friend who is a clergyman in the Anglican Church who became a priest at the age of about 28 - a young man. His wife is also a priest. Before becoming a priest, he loved being part of church; he had lots of friends. But since being a clergyman, he noticed that if he invited people round for a meal, he often was not invited back, and felt it wasn't because he put people off when they came round! It seemed that people did not want to invite him (and his wife) because people felt they could not really relax with them, as they were their priests. In other words, people did not want to risk their reputation when relaxed with their pastors!

The tragedy of this situation, apart from the isolation of our Christian leaders, is that it represents an idolatry of the self. Who cares what your priest thinks of you! Isn't it what God thinks of you that matters? He knows everything about you and still loves you with an unconditional, forgiving love. If you

[5] Although versions of this statement are attributed to many other people too.

believe that, why do you care what other people in your church think? Why do we worry what other Christians think of us? Why do we present this false image of ourselves if not because we are idolising our image and reputation? To let go of this is to experience a true release, a joy in our salvation.

ii) Doubt: we can be faced with doubt however committed we have been and however convicted we have been. Some doubt because they become depressed or downhearted by their situation, as John may have felt. Some doubt because things have not worked out as they hoped or expected, as may have been the case for John, because he may have known Jesus was the long-waited-for Messiah but did not understand what that meant. In our youth we fantasise about how our lives might pan out, and these fantasies are our hopes. It is not realistic to expect our narcissistic fantasies to all be fulfilled, and spiritually it would probably be very bad for most of us. God calls us to the life he wants for us, with sacrifices, hard work, sometimes mundane, sometimes exciting, sometimes recognised, sometimes thankless.

Our doubts are part of our faith. Perhaps the people who doubt least are those who have invested least in their faith. Their doubt is superficial and does not cause distress because their faith is superficial. Let us embrace doubt as a painful but potentially enriching part of faith, the reverse side of which coin is a committed faith.

iii) Disappointment: another striking aspect of John's feelings in Luke 7 is that John seems disappointed in Jesus' ministry. Disappointment is a dangerous emotion that can eat away at us and be a source of real spiritual depression. The definition of disappointment is an expectation which is not met. From this definition, it is clear that the key aspect of disappointment is our expectation. For John, he expected Jesus to be different; perhaps he hoped he would be more active in opposing Roman rule, we do not know exactly. Most faithful Jewish people expected the Messiah to restore or cleanse the Temple, defeat the enemy and bring God's justice, ushering in the Kingdom of God. Jesus' vision of this Messiahship was radically different and maybe John was just not on his wavelength. How extraordinary it seems to us that John, of all people, could be disappointed in Jesus' ministry, a ministry and teaching that has inspired so many for two thousand years and a life that is easily the most influential in human history. But disappointed he was, and that should warn us of the danger of disappointment. Our expectations are determined by our own limited perspective. We need to be wary of our expectations and have humility. What we expect of our spouse, our children, our pastor or our church needs to be tempered with humility. Many are damaged because their expectations of others far exceed what the other can deliver and is far greater than their expectations of themselves. How many people drive their children away because they are disappointed that their children have not met the fantasy they have for them, which is often a fulfilment of things they were unable to do themselves? How many people leave a church in disappointment that it is not filled with better Christians than themselves? Our expectations need to be generous, humble, realistic, hopeful but not binding. And remember, others will find us disappointing.

Reflection

As a psychiatrist, several times I had patients say after the first consultation, 'It is so good to find a decent psychiatrist who listens to me. All the others I have seen have let me down'. I soon learned to see this not as a compliment but as a predictor that I would not meet their expectations, because I am not better at my job than most psychiatrists, I have my strengths and weaknesses as do all my colleagues. Towards the end of my career, I would reply along the lines of, 'Thanks, but I think you may find me as human and disappointing as the other psychiatrists you have seen, I will do my best but I will let you down at times, as we all let each other down at times'.

To be a disappointment is hurtful, but we must not let the expectations of others determine our behaviour. Our behaviour needs to be determined by the love of God.

iv) Death: finally, from the story of John the Baptiser let us remember that life does not always end well. This is painful but should not be a cause of anguish. As a young doctor I saw people die and had to certify those who had passed away. Often it is a rather sudden and shocking event, made messy by those who, quite reasonably, are trying to prevent it. At other times it is prolonged over days, without a clear 'moment' of death, but drawn out, full of confusion often caused by pain-killing medication. It is not as in the films, neat with lots of emotionally satisfying goodbyes. And that is OK. Most of the disciples, like John, had violent, unpleasant deaths. God wants us to live our lives as well as we can, and how they end is not up to us. Let us accept this and not be anxious about how we die but concerned about how we live.

In this John has set us a fine and honest example to follow.

Chapter 5

Understanding forgiveness and repentance: combating guilt and shame.

Forgive us our debts, as we forgive the debts of others.
(Matthew 6:12 NIV)

Guilt is a core psychological symptom of clinical depression. Many secular psychologists and psychiatrists accuse religious faith of inducing mental illness by promoting feelings of guilt. In contrast, I feel the Christian understanding of guilt and forgiveness offers enormous solace and a way of recovery from the emotion of guilt, but we need a mature and deep understanding of guilt and forgiveness to reach the cleansing benefits of dealing with guilt. Others have written at length on a Christian understanding of guilt, and I would recommend a recent book authored by a priest and a psychiatrist entitled *The Guilt Book* (van der Hart and Waller, 2014).

True guilt

Firstly, it is important to acknowledge that there can be false guilt and true guilt. True guilt is the acknowledgement of moral wrongdoing in which genuinely negative moral acts have been admitted and evaluated. Clearly a crucial aspect of true guilt is the judgement of whether an act is genuinely negative or not, and therefore there can be a blurring of lines between true guilt and false guilt. Within a Christian worldview, the Christian conscience is influenced by biblical interpretation of what is genuinely good and genuinely bad in moral behaviour. We underestimate how important it is for us individually and as a society to be clear about what is good and bad morally. A healthy Christian conscience has its roots in biblical teaching and the inspiration of the Holy Spirit, and therefore has an objective rationality as well as an emotional response.

True guilt is the consequence of bad things we have done - a matter of moral judgement. From a Christian perspective, we have all sinned and fallen short of the glory of God. True guilt and false guilt can overlap, as people can be overwhelmed and paralysed by guilt for the things they have done wrong and this paralysis leads to accusations from the secular world that religious faith engenders neurosis and mental illness. The other side of this coin is that the secular understanding of guilt has few frameworks for moral judgement, but patients suffering from true guilt for failings in their lives desperately want a way to deal with their guilt, and this is something that secular therapies struggle to provide. It is here that the Christian ideas of repentance and forgiveness have a great power.

Reflection

I remember talking with a man with a severe schizophrenic illness. Many people with severe schizophrenia become concrete in their thinking and struggle to understand the complexity of social relationships. He had made sexual advances to his sister (when both were adults). She was horrified and their relationship was broken. When he told me this he was wracked by guilt and totally heartbroken; their relationship was blighted. He had real remorse for his actions but had nowhere to take this true guilt. I felt heartbroken for him. This was many years ago and I cannot remember what I advised, but now I would advise him, if he was willing, to speak to the excellent mental health chaplains we have available to talk about confession, repentance and forgiveness, if not in that overtly religious language. Many of my patients agree to do so, some do not because they do not feel this is appropriate. We need somewhere to take our true guilt, which is ultimately to God. The Bible advises us to confess our sins to each other (James 5:16).

One way of dealing with true guilt without recourse to religious faith is through denial and diminishing the consequences of our wrong actions. In its mildest form this often involves the statement, 'It's not a big deal'. When most extreme this attitude leads to psychopathy, when people suppress all sense of guilt. It can result in severe brutalisation and the dehumanising of others. People can emotionally, physically and sexually abuse others with little sense of guilt. This is not uncommon - ask any psychiatrist, psychologist or social worker in any town in England. I would argue it is endemic in all societies.

Christianity is quite extreme. Jesus often said things that are extremely demanding: give everything you have to the poor; you must (by comparison) hate your mother and your father for my sake; it is harder for the rich man to go through the eye of a needle than to enter the kingdom of God; whoever looks at a woman lustfully has committed adultery in his heart; if someone punches you on one side of the face, offer him the other side to punch.

We have tended in our weaker moments to take the extreme demands of Christianity and either water them down or use them to condemn people. But Jesus actually condemns very few people. He often surprises everyone by forgiving them, without the person obviously repenting. Perhaps what we need to accept is that the ideal that God sets for us is not a hurdle to get over (and we condemn people when they fail) but a goal we can set ourselves and strive to achieve, accepting that we will have regular failures and setbacks but that we should not compromise by changing the ideal. That is why forgiveness is vital. There is no cancel culture in Christ, but the truth of the ideal should not be compromised either.

False guilt

False guilt is based less on moral judgement and more on emotional feelings. It is 'typically experienced as persistent and distressing guilty feelings' (van der Hart and Waller, 2014). It can lack objectivity, as our rational minds can be overwhelmed by rampant negative emotions. It can present without a moral cause and can distort our perception of reality and our relationships. It can lead to shame, in which our guilty feelings come to represent our whole personhood. This can be a significant source of depression.

Reflection

I noticed quite early in my adult life that my sense of guilt was much more linked to being found out than to the wrong act itself. If something I had done which was wrong was unnoticed, I would feel a little guilty about it, but when it became public my sense of guilt and shame would rocket. It struck me that I was more concerned with my reputation than with my true moral state. This is a battle I still have to fight and it has made me try to tell people of my wrongdoings, so I do not minimise them, whilst also reducing any sense of shame at being found out. This is why I think 'confessing our sins to one another' is a good idea as it brings a sense of relief that our failures are known but we are not rejected. I would not want to tell anyone and everyone, but telling a trusted person has a profound benefit.

Some false guilt is a product of delusional thinking, when someone is racked by a sense of guilt based on false beliefs or an exaggerated interpretation of events. Clearly this is a misinterpretation of reality, and people who are delusional lose the ability to assess reality accurately.

People can be prone to false guilt about obsessional thoughts, including when depressed and those who suffer obsessive-compulsive disorder. There is some evidence that people of faith are especially prone to obsessional thoughts. These are unpleasant or obscene thoughts that are intrusive. People will often try to resist these thoughts, which makes them more intrusive and hence more distressing.

Van der Hart and Waller describe how people, especially Christians, can cope with false guilt through self-defeating behaviours. These include searching for reasons for guilty feelings, avoidance, compulsive confession, rumination, perfectionism and self-punishment. Many Christians try to understand why their lives are not as successful as they might be by trying to find some sin that explains this. This goes back to a pagan view of God - if life is difficult, he must be punishing us. The 'health and wealth' gospel is a false gospel that feeds into this pagan view of God.

Reflection

Mike is a hard-working nurse in the local hospital. He is desperate for promotion as he lives in a relatively small house and has three growing children, one of whom suffers from mild autism. He keeps going for promotion but misses out because he struggles to get higher qualifications such as a Master's degree. His church is relatively affluent, and he sees fellow Christians being more successful in their careers and earning more than him. At times he feels spiritually inferior and feels guilty that he does not pray more, does not have time to be a leader in the church and cannot give as much money as others. He feels these may be the reasons for his lack of career progress, that God is somehow not blessing him. Sometimes he feels angry with God, but this makes him feel more guilty. Beth, his wife, finds his gloominess frustrating and keeps reassuring him that the family are happy, they just want him to spend time with them and relax, something he finds it hard to do. He talks with the vicar. She tells Mike that she knows colleagues in the hospital who say he is a fantastic nurse who is great with patients. That is more important than all the money in the world. Mike struggles to believe her. She suggests he might seek a spiritual mentor he can talk with regularly.

Mature reflection, perhaps with a thoughtful and experienced spiritual mentor or director, helps to expose these self-defeating coping behaviours. Perfectionism is a particular trap Christians can get caught up in as they consider Christ's words:

Be perfect, just as your Father in heaven is perfect.
(Matthew 5: 38)

Van der Hart and Waller point out that this passage can be translated, *Be complete, just as your Father in heaven is complete*. We are only made complete through the forgiveness of God - a gift of grace - and we need to accept this gift and not expect to achieve it by ourselves.

<u>Repentance and forgiveness</u>

Abbot Christopher Jamison (2008) distinguishes between 'feeling guilty' and 'being guilty'. If our response to being guilty stops at just feeling guilty, it can become a neurotic self-absorption or a fear of being found out. If feeling guilty does not lead to action it can be truly neurotic, and Jamison identifies this as the traditional 'Catholic guilt' that is often criticised by the secular world - justifiably.

He goes on to say that the true Catholic tradition does not stop at 'feeling guilty'- it progresses to action. This is 'justifiable guilt'- genuine remorse for real wrongdoing - and is a prelude to real growth. It leads to repentance - a turning around, a change of direction, a change of behaviour. Repentance of an action is a commitment not to do it in the future. This leads to personal growth. Note that repentance is an act, a behaviour, not a feeling. However, our actions are often determined by our feelings, hence we need to be mindful of both.

Of course, the Christian view of guilt, remorse and repentance does not start with us, it starts with God. There is a popular view that the Old Testament God is somewhat different to the New Testament God, the former full of judgement, the latter full of love. Most readers will know that this is not true. Listen to the psalmist in Psalm 103:

The Lord is merciful and gracious, slow to anger and abundant in loving kindness. He will not always accuse, neither will he stay angry for ever. He has not dealt with us according to our sins, nor repaid us for our iniquities...As far as the east is from the west, so far has he removed our transgressions from us.

(vs 8-12, NIV)

Remember that this was written centuries before the death and resurrection of Jesus Christ. God's revelation has forgiveness at its heart and this is good news for the guilty (all of us) because it gives us hope.

Guilt is therefore addressed through repentance and forgiveness by God, but Jesus, in what has become known as the Lord's prayer, links our forgiveness with our willingness to forgive others. My goodness, that is a challenge. As we perhaps realise more as we grow older, forgiving others is a lot easier in theory than in practice. As C.S. Lewis remarked, we all believe in forgiveness until we have to do it. Yet we also know that bitterness and resentment eat away at ourselves, not the person we feel anger towards, and forgiveness releases us as well as someone who has grieved us. Therefore, in this small sentence, Christ both lays down a severe challenge to us, and also gives us the pathway to freedom - freedom not just from bitterness but from a significant source of depression. In repentance and forgiveness, we have a source of joy we can trust.

Chapter 6

Clearing our minds: combating unhealthy fantasies.

'You have heard that it was said to the people long ago, "You shall not murder, and anyone who murders will be subject to judgment." But I tell you that anyone who is angry with a brother or sister will be subject to judgment. You have heard that it was said, "You shall not commit adultery." But I tell you that anyone who looks at a woman lustfully has already committed adultery with her in his heart.

(Matthew 5: 21-22, 27-28 NIV)

And he said unto his disciples, 'Therefore I say unto you: Take no thought for your life, what ye shall eat; neither for the body, what ye shall put on. The life is more than meat, and the body is more than raiment. Consider the ravens: for they neither sow nor reap; which neither have storehouse nor barn; and God feedeth them: how much more are ye better than the fowls? And which of you with taking thought can add to his stature one cubit? If ye then be not able to do that thing which is least, why take ye thought for the rest? Consider the lilies how they grow: they toil not, they spin not; and yet I say unto you, that Solomon in all his glory was not arrayed like one of these. If then God so clothe the grass, which is today in the field, and tomorrow is cast into the oven; how much more will he clothe you, O ye of little faith? And seek not ye what ye shall eat, or what ye shall drink, neither be ye of doubtful mind. For all these things do the nations of the world seek after: and your Father knoweth that ye have need of these things. But rather seek ye the kingdom of God; and all these things shall be added unto you. Fear not, little flock; for it is your Father's good pleasure to give you the kingdom.

(Luke 12: 22-32 KJV)

Reflection

I have a personality that needs to be angry about something. If I do not have a 'cause' to fight for, I feel a bit restless and bored. As a result, I am often fighting some battle, usually at work, that I believe is justified. And as a result of that, I am often at loggerheads with someone. I am aware that I imagine many arguments with people whom I do not agree with and have often fantasied about arguments in which I imagine others saying things they have never said. I feel my red-hot anger rising inside me (for some reason this often happens when I am driving). I can be like this for many minutes until I realise I am furious with someone for something they have never said; I have just made them say it in my head! My anger fantasy has made me hate them for those few minutes (and I confess, sometimes longer).

How we think affects both how we feel and how we act. Jesus' observations are telling us these truths and are consistent with cognitive theories of depression developed over the last four decades which are put into practice in cognitive behavioural therapy. Cognitive therapy is a type of psychotherapy in which negative patterns of thought about the self and the world are challenged. Jesus examined how we think in the above passages and focussed on anger, lust and anxiety. I would suggest that these challenging areas are as relevant as ever and have become more challenging with the development of the internet.

It strikes me that discussions around fantasies about lust and anger have a certain moralistic tone whereas anxious fantasies are seen more as a mental health issue. Nevertheless, I strongly feel that all these fantasies have significant impact on our spiritual lives.

i) Lust: people have always been susceptible to lustful thoughts. We are sexual beings and created as such by God. We are called to be faithful to our spouses but are attracted to other people. To be faithful is to be grateful to God and our spouse for the sexual lives we share, and adultery breaks bonds of trust that enrich not only ourselves and our spouses but also our children who benefit so much from a strong relationship between their parents.

Infidelity does not start in the bedroom: it starts in our minds. If we find someone else attractive, we can fantasise that their personality will match their physical attractiveness. Through ignorance of the admired person, we can overlook their faults… while we intimately know the flaws in our spouses. Our fantasy of that person can out-score the reality of our spouse. Jesus is right in observing that unfaithfulness starts in our imagination, and it is here we can be disciplined in nipping sexual fantasies in the bud by challenging the falsehood of our mind's distortions. In this we prevent catastrophic mistakes.

The internet makes pornography so easy to access, and many men and women are tempted to look at it. The fantasies it feeds can fuel a lack of gratitude to a spouse and the consequences can be a growing resentment that our partners do not live up to impossible demands in our minds. It is so important to face this challenge. People need to be supported to overcome any shame they feel about seeking and receiving help. If King David succumbed to visual temptation, it is not surprising that we can. If we can control our minds, it is so much easier to master our actions.

ii) Anger: it is easier to consider sexual fantasies more grievous than fantasies of anger, but I suspect angry fantasies cause as much suffering, if not more, than sexual fantasies. I described at the beginning of this chapter how I can fantasise arguments with people I am in conflict with. I imagine arguments and of course always have the upper hand in my well-thought-out scenarios. The more disturbing aspect is me putting words in their mouths that are a product of my mind, not theirs. Yet I can hate them for those words, as I described above. I am aware that my personality is such that I want to be in some kind of battle without which I tend to get bored. This can lead me to fighting some good causes, but at other times I can get sucked into trivial issues which do not justify my anger. We need to check our fantasies and remember to evaluate people on reality and not our imagination. In this Jesus was surely right in calling us not to murder people in our own heads.

Reflection

The new phenomenon of complete strangers threatening people on Twitter or the internet for trivial reasons may be a reflection of this. Recently, in the UK, a feminist journalist campaigned for Jane Austen, the great Victorian writer, to be represented on the five-pound note. To most people this seems a reasonable and hardly controversial desire. As a result, however, she received alarming messages from people: vitriolic anger and threats of rape. When these so-called 'trolls' were detected, some were women.

It seems people can become furious in their fantasies, and, if they think they can remain anonymous, are willing to terrorise others in a very distressing manner.

iii) Anxiety about the future: I could not resist using the King James Version for the text from Luke concerning anxiety. There are few more beautiful passages in the English language than this translation of Jesus' teaching. The beauty of the words, worthy of Shakespeare, mirror Jesus' appreciation of the beauty of the natural world, which he has clearly reflected on deeply.

Reflection

Where I have lived in Cornwall, every spring there is a timed display of wildflowers in the hedgerows, beginning with snowdrops, then bluebells, wild garlic, primroses, pink and red valerian. It is a stunning display of the spontaneous diversity of the created world, and worthy of this passage. I wonder if seeing it each year helps me combat my anxieties - I suspect it does.

Anxiety is closely linked to depression and many people experience both together and indeed they can seem to feed each other, leading to a vicious spiral into illness.

Christ's teaching on anxiety predates cognitive therapy by a couple of millennia but has some striking similarities. He tells us not to focus on worries about the future which cannot change that future, but to live in the now which we can affect. Our beliefs about the future are inherently fantasies- our imagination running riot. We can spend time and emotional effort worrying about the future which does not change anything. We need discipline to break ourselves out of these mental cul-de-sacs. Many of our concerns about the future are negative fantasies which may never happen, and so we are worrying unnecessarily. Sometimes we need to distract ourselves by doing something useful in the present to stop these thought processes from gaining traction.

Reflection

Consider this scenario: Alison has been prone to depression and anxiety all her life. Her parents were similarly prone to anxiety and Alison was always over-protected and warned of all possible bad outcomes in life. She has recently been transferred from one department of the local council to another due to a reorganisation. This has sent her anxiety into orbit. She continuously talks to her husband about how she does not know if she will get on with her new boss and whether new colleagues will like her. As a result, she goes off sick in the first week of the redeployment. Now she worries what everyone will think of her work ethic. She sees a psychologist from the mental health team, who suggests cognitive behavioural therapy for her anxiety. Alison tries to understand how her beliefs about the future are causing her anxiety and hampering her functioning in the here and now.

To break these thought cycles is easier said than done. But Christ also adds something to his teaching that is not included in secular cognitive therapy: that is, a meditation on our dependence on God and his faithfulness to us. Our lack of faith is a source of anxiety, and we are called to build our faith in God in order to combat our anxiety. Faith is like a muscle - if we don't use it, it will atrophy and become weak. We are called to practice our faith in order to build it up and then our anxiety can diminish. That is why we need to engage with faith communities and be active in our faith - taking risks for God. Individualistic faith can easily become self-referent, self-obsessed and prone to anxiety.

The fundamental emotion of anxiety is fear, and how many times in the Bible are we told, 'Do not be afraid'? I have read it is 365 times! Yet this seems easier to say than to do. How do we exercise our faith to avoid fear? One way is to realise that avoidance of the feared situation increases our tendency to anxiety. With phobias, avoidance of the feared object increases the anxiety, and the mainstay of treatment is exposure and response prevention. In agoraphobia, there is a fear of places without an easy exit - trains, buses, supermarkets on a busy Friday evening. To overcome this, we need to gradually expose sufferers to situations that raise anxiety and encourage them to stick with it until their anxiety diminishes and the fantasy of catastrophe is shown to be untrue.

We live in a risk-averse society, when safety can be everything, and risk taking unacceptable. In some situations, such as aviation, this is to be most welcomed. But in others it is paralysing. Spiritually we can fear taking risks and especially fear failure, interpreting it as a sign of sin, the lack of God's blessing or even a judgement from God. I would argue that Christian communities that never do things that fail are probably avoiding risks and the consequences of failure, and therefore failing to exercise faith. Christ calls us not to fear, to step out in faith and take risks - and it will be this that builds our faith. After all, on the surface he had failures. Many of his followers left him because his teaching was too hard. People were not healed in Nazareth because they were too familiar with him and could not believe he was someone special. At his death, his best friends abandoned him. Jesus knew failure and embraced it as a consequence of following God. For Christian communities, it is important to be constantly stepping outside our comfort zones, doing new things, meeting new people, individually and collectively. Some of these things will not work out, but some will and we will only get new successes if we accept new failures and trust God.

So, to summarise: We always need to be bold in stepping out in faith, to embrace spiritual risks in following God's call. As we exercise our faith, our spiritual muscles will grow, and anxieties will diminish as we refuse to avoid feared situations.

Another great antidote to anxiety and depression is gratitude.

I shall say more about this in the final chapter.

Chapter 7

Understanding what we need: combating the desire for more.

I rejoiced greatly in the Lord that at last you renewed your concern for me. Indeed, you were concerned, but you had no opportunity to show it. I am not saying this because I am in need, for I have learned to be content whatever the circumstances. I know what it is to be in need, and I know what it is to have plenty. I have learned the secret of being content in any and every situation, whether well fed or hungry, whether living in plenty or in want. I can do all this through him who gives me strength.

(Philippians 4: 10-13 NIV)

The tendency to compare ourselves to others is an extremely powerful reflex and is generally destructive. I have compared myself to my brother, my fellow pupils at school, fellow medical students and doctors, neighbours, friends and people at church. I notice that it is easy to compare ourselves spiritually to others in a destructive fashion as much as it is for more material comparisons. It leads to envy, resentment, self-pity and even hatred. Parents can also project this desire to compare on to their children, seeing their relative success as a reflection on their own status.

Since Martyn Lloyd-Jones delivered his sermons on spiritual depression at Westminster Chapel in 1964, society in the

United Kingdom has changed in many ways. One of the most significant is a greater inequality in wealth. Disparities between the rich and the poor are growing, as described in *The Spirit Level* by economists Wilkinson and Pickett (2010). Whilst materialism has been a big motivational driver in western societies for many decades, between 1918 and 1979 society in the UK became more equal in wealth. Unfortunately, this has reversed in the last 40 years, although data can show some variation in this trend. The striking evidence from *The Spirit Level* is that greater inequality makes people in a society less happy, both the poor and the rich. It is fascinating how modern social science supports the ideas, found in the biblical narrative, of justice delivering peace, or shalom.

The temptation to accumulate wealth and possessions has been present in all of human history, as evidenced in the command given by God over 3000 years ago not to covet our neighbours' possessions. But our desire to possess more than others is not just limited to wealth.

Wanting more than others - the desire for supremacy

My view concerning the desire for more possessions is that it is part of the more primal drive for supremacy, a desire for omnipotence and replacing God with ourselves. Treating all human beings as equal, all in the image of God, is a great virtue worth striving for, but hard to live up to. The serpent in the garden of Eden told Eve that God did not want rivals and if she ate the apple she would be like God. The serpent fed into the desire for human beings to replace God with themselves. As a result, we rank ourselves and others in order of importance and significance. After all, if we want omnipotence, we do not want to share the power with others. How we do this, consciously or unconsciously, will determine how we rank ourselves. We are constantly tempted to seek omnipotence, even though this is strikingly impossible to achieve.

How we compete: money, sex and power.

Our culture can rank people not only by how much wealth they have but also according to other significant idols - how attractive they look, how successful they are in their work or field of endeavour, how popular and how influential. For people who are known for their attractiveness, growing older can be a painful process. I am struck by how many extraordinarily attractive film stars and models have surgery to look younger even though they are still very attractive as they age (and actually look far worse as a result of their surgery). In academic circles, levels of success count highly, in academic output and status. I notice how difficult retirement can be for those with a successful medical career - their identity is invested in their career success and status to an unhealthy degree.

Reflection

I have recently semi-retired. After 32 years of clinical work, I felt quite burnt out and was really happy to finish the job I was doing. However, I soon realised that I kept checking my emails. Whereas I used to get angry and frustrated at the number of emails I was sent, now I felt sad that I was not needed so much and that my opinion on decisions was less urgently sought. To let go of that status was, and is, difficult. I am still working for the NHS and enjoy this but know my influence is dwindling - which is painful but necessary, for the service and for me. Life incorporates 'dying' to former selves, with the grief involved, whilst new things are born.

Ranking by wealth now has a rival in ranking by popularity. Many young people idolise their own significance on social media. Lloyd-Jones remarked in 1964, how difficult it had become not to be organised by the world he lived in, through television, radio and the media. He remarked on the 'boredom of the blackout' in the second world war - how people struggled with no electricity and a lack of stimulation from radio. My goodness, how things have accelerated! Now we notice how families in cafes and restaurants can all be looking at their mobile phones. I notice (and I am guilty of this myself) that if I am in a talk or meeting at work, and it is a little boring, how tempting it is to look on our mobile devices. Many of us openly answer emails in meetings. The levels of stimulation we feel we need are extraordinary. And when any of our categories of significance are threatened as they can be, especially with illness, are we content; are we sufficient in God? We need to be - that is what Paul is saying - to give us resilience in the face of a world which says our value is in our attractiveness, our status, how wanted we are, how many 'hits' we get, the number of followers we have on Twitter, the number of friends on Facebook, how much we earn, what we own. These are all lies. They do not satisfy: and these drives can lead to depression because we never get enough to really satisfy a desire for more as we never achieve omnipotence. The idea of 'enough' is so important for our mental health. There is such a thing as enough - enough money, enough possessions, enough friends, enough status.

The idolisation of spiritual 'success'.

We must be wary because these idolatries can infiltrate the church - we can rank people by the quality of their personality and selflessness of their lives in a way that generates competitive envy and spiritual narcissism. Within church communities, envy and desire for influence can easily corrupt communities. We can compare pastors and priests and rank their talents and virtues. How good are they at growing the church? Who is the best preacher? We can judge each other in church communities by how much we do for the church community, not accounting for the other responsibilities people have, often unseen. We can be particularly unfair in judging parents by how their children develop, with consequent bitterness and resentment from children if they perceive they are being used as tokens of spiritual success by their parents rather than being loved for themselves.

The goodness of creation: the material world is good.

This is not to argue for asceticism. Beauty is a gift from God. The beauty of the human body is a wonderful gift from God, as is our sexuality. It should be enjoyed but not idolised or abused. The beauty of things created is expressed many times in the Bible, and the creativity of art is participating in God's work. It is notable how much of the book of Exodus is taken up with God guiding the artistic endeavour of designing the tabernacle. It is wonderful to enjoy good food and admire good design. The vision of a feast is a common promise of God to his people in the Bible. It is the dependence on these things that can pull us down into depression.

The cure: sufficiency in God

Martyn Lloyd-Jones (1998) focussed on the above passage in Philippians to stress the importance of being content in all circumstances. He identifies that Paul is 'self-sufficient, independent of circumstances, independent of surroundings, independent of conditions' (p.277). Now this is a vital point. To be joyful, we need to be dependent on one thing only- the love of God. To be dependent on anything else makes us vulnerable to depression because other things are not ultimately satisfying or life-giving. We must not become dependent on our status, our wealth or our attractiveness. Even where they are present, our dependence on them leads to envy, narcissism, self-obsession and meaninglessness.

Paul was content because he had learned not to be reliant on these things but to be in a similar state of being when having very little or being well provided for. He could clearly mix with the rich and powerful, the intellectual elite, or with the poor and those who are not blessed with education or exalted intelligence. He was not actually self-sufficient. He was sufficient in God.

There is a danger of interpreting this as a justification of inequality which it is not - justice for the poor is a common cry in scripture. Shalom is a key concept in the Hebrew testament. This does not just mean peace but a peace with justice and wholeness. Scottish theologian Jim Punton (1977) describes shalom as 'speaking of a totally integrated life with health of body, heart and mind, attuned to nature, open to others, in joy with God: of sharing, mutuality and love: of justice, freedom, interdependence and reciprocity' (p.1). The peace or shalom of God depends on justice and we are to work for the justice and shalom of God in this life in the here and now. Nor is our position on not seeking wealth denigrating the goodness of ambition and hard work which can generate wealth and do much good for many. Being content in all things is not about passivity and laziness. It is about our spiritual state of mind being independent of these things.

We are valuable to God and no more or no less valuable than any other human being on earth. William Temple said our religion is what we are in our solitude[6] and being sufficient in all

[6] Widely attributed : see https://www.goodreads.com/author/quotes/397351.William_Temple

circumstances leads to true joy and keeps us resilient to combat depression.

Chapter 8

Understanding our sexuality: advocating fidelity to support attachment.

Like an apple tree among the trees of the forest
is my beloved among the young men.
I delight to sit in his shade,
and his fruit is sweet to my taste.
Let him lead me to the banquet hall,
and let his banner over me be love.
Strengthen me with raisins,
refresh me with apples,
for I am faint with love.
His left arm is under my head,
and his right arm embraces me.
Daughters of Jerusalem, I charge you
by the gazelles and by the does of the field:
Do not arouse or awaken love
until it so desires.

(Song of Songs 2: 3-7, NIV)

There is something that the Christian church and Freud have in common: both have been accused of being obsessed with sex. Both may have made mistakes in their understanding of sexuality but both may be right in understanding the sheer magnitude of the effect sexual desire can have on our lives, and the importance of how we express our sexuality to our emotional wellbeing.

It has always struck me how the aspects of our lives which can be the most powerful forces for good and happiness can also inflict the most damage upon us, and thus be a source of significant depression. Sexuality is the case in point, but it is also true in our relationship with our parents, our relationship with money, how we view power and life within the church. All can be tremendous forces for good, and all can inflict terrible harm. However, we must be wary not to polarise the forces within them - our sexual lives are rarely close to pure and thankfully few are utterly brutal. Most churches seek to do good, but inadvertently can advocate doctrines and practices that distort truly healthy lives.

It is easy to criticise the attitude of the Church to sex, but the church should always speak up about how we should live our sexual lives because it is so important. We need to talk about it, debate it and wrestle with it. Currently the temptation is to keep quiet for fear of offending or excluding each other: engagement in difficult discussions is absolutely necessary. The debate around the theology and ethics of same-sex relationships is deeply personal to many and can polarise easily. Terrible abuses of children and adults by people in authority within the church have also led to justifiable guilt and a wish to avoid the subject. But we must be open and transparent about institutional and individual sins and failures whilst still wrestling with and teaching God's word on his created world. Glyn Harrison, a fellow psychiatrist, has published an excellent apologetic for an orthodox position on Christian sexuality entitled, *A Better Story*. He correctly, in my view, observes that the sexual revolution of the late twentieth century was caused by the repression of sexuality within the church over centuries. Because sexuality was put in an unhealthy straight jacket, when people threw off the tight, repressive bonds, a chaotic and damaging expression of sexuality has been the result. Harrison goes on to argue that the advocacy of faithful sexual lives should not just be a theological and philosophical defence but a strong narrative of joy: a better story.

Sex and depression

As a psychiatrist, the effects of our sexual lives on our mental health, have always been evident. Childhood sexual abuse is a massive cause of depression, although we must not be despairing about this matter- people who have been sexually abused in childhood can and do live fulfilling and rich lives, often free from depression and mental illness. Trauma can lead to mental illness but in the majority of people does not do so. For those who do develop depression due to past abuse, that illness is very treatable and healing is possible. People do recover from depression caused by childhood sexual abuse. But the damage done to people should never be underestimated and perpetrators should be brought to justice. For every child abused there is an adult who has failed to control their sexual desires.

Broken sexual relationships in adulthood are also a massive source of depression. Rob Bell (2007) describes how falling in love is an act of opening ourselves up, giving power to someone else, as God opens himself up to us. If that opening up leads to rejection, the broken heartedness is extremely painful. Few of us have not experienced that sense of rejection to some extent. Sexual restraint is there to protect us from that pain, to limit it. When sexual intimacy is advocated for committed relationships only, it is to protect us from the pain of rejection and also to protect and emphasise the special, exclusive nature of that relationship. It amplifies the love in that relationship and binds us closer together. I believe that the reason that, in the Bible, sex is advocated for lifelong commitment is not because of the problem with sex outside this context, but with the problem of a sexual relationship being ended by one party, leaving the other devastated and broken by rejection.

Celibacy and loneliness

Reflection:

I was married for 16 years but have spent significant periods of my adult life celibate. Before meeting my future wife, I was always anxious about my ability to maintain a relationship as I am by nature quite solitudinous. I am actually sociable and enjoy the company of most people, but after three or four hours I want to say, "It's been great seeing you, cheerio!" One of the reasons I knew I loved my wife was that I could spend more than a few hours with her and didn't want her to go! I am sorry if that sounds rather selfish, but it is true. Hopefully she felt the same way about me.

Since the death of my wife, I am not concerned with that anxiety, but loneliness is more of an issue because I miss her. I did get lonely at times in my younger single years but found being active and having friends often cured that loneliness. And I know many people in relationships feel desperately lonely because their partner does not or cannot fulfil their expectations.

This is not the book for a detailed analysis of celibacy, but I will say that I have always disliked any over-emphasis on the primacy of marriage and parenthood in the Christian church. Marriage is a God-given blessing, but we are all aware that Jesus was single as, probably, was Paul. Although I do not think the institutional celibacy of the priesthood is either biblical or healthy, there is a long-held practice of chosen celibacy in the monastic tradition and the individual's choice of celibacy can be wonderfully life-affirming. Where it is part of the un-chosen facts of anyone's life, an associated loneliness and hunger for intimacy can lead to depression. The church should be a place where singleness is recognised for its challenges and its joys and is fully supported and strongly valued whether in community or in a more solitudinous approach to life.

I offer no easy answers in this or any other situation, including less than happy marriages when people are no longer connecting with each other. I am very aware of the diversity in personalities of people of faith. There is no prescriptive way: we can seek God's calling and have the courage to follow it. Some people find community and friendship challenging and enjoy solitude, others are social animals who thrive in company and need community.

I do believe that seeking a closer relationship with God is key. Being active in our faith, together and on our own, helps us to lean into God. Leaning into God in marriage or in celibacy helps mitigate against pain, heal wounds and offers sources of joy, happiness, strength and vision which can be channelled into activities and relationships which give shape and meaning to our lives.

Sex and exclusivity

Sex is usually very enjoyable. This is not surprising as it was created by God to be so. It is a gift from God. Most of us are attracted to a lot of people. Again, this is not surprising as God created us to be beautiful, sexually attractive to others. This is especially true when we are young adults, but, surprisingly to the young, tends to persist! We are called to be sexual people, but in order to protect us from the depression of a broken heart, and to increase the goodness of a committed sexual relationship (which is about a lot more than sex), we are called to sexual restraint through sexual exclusiveness, and the ideal is one fully sexual relationship until one of the couple leaves this life. We call this marriage for convenient communication. This protects us from a broken heart and depression.

Why is sexual love exclusive? Friendship is not, we share friendship, we do not demand exclusivity. Of course, some people see sexuality in a similar way, with multiple partners and open relationships. It is interesting that in an increasingly secular society in which pornography is often accepted as normal, relatively few people openly adopt this lifestyle. Adultery, whilst clearly happening as it always has, is seen generally as a bad thing for us. Most people with no belief in God still long for an exclusive, committed sexual relationship. Some would argue that, from an evolutionary perspective, this is because it is better for children, and there is good evidence to back this up. Whilst many children now live in families with mothers and fathers in separate relationships, the ideal of a good marriage is stubbornly popular - if difficult to achieve.

Reflection

The Rocky Horror Picture Show is an iconic musical premiered in 1973 that has captured the public imagination. It mocks the naive and boring couple, Brad and Janet, who are seduced by the charismatic transvestite bisexual, Frank Enfurter. Frank advocates the pursuit of unrestrained pleasure whilst pouring contempt on fidelity to one partner. However, even in this show, the character Columbia suddenly turns on Frank, declaring herself heartbroken because she loved him but he used her before discarding her as he was continuing to do to others. In the stage production I saw, she is only silenced by effectively being drugged, anaesthetising her feelings of rejection and brokenness. Even in this sexually permissive production, the underlying problem of sexual libertarianism is acknowledged - lasting damage to attachments. The permissive society facilitates the use and abuse of others to gratify ourselves. The show ends by describing people as insects walking on the planet, living a meaningless existence. I believe this philosophy has had a hugely damaging effect on western societies.

Society seems to be denying the overwhelming evidence of the damage done by unrestrained sexuality. Infidelity damages relationships and damages children. The importance of attachment to our psychological welfare strongly directs us towards fidelity. Attachment is fundamentally important within sexual relationships as well as between parents and children.

Attachment is an important concept in psychology, developed by the psychiatrist and psychoanalyst John Bowlby in the second half of the twentieth century. The attachment between a child and a parent figure, usually but not always the mother, in the first three years of life is seen as crucial in our ability to trust others and feel secure in relationships. This gives us a solid foundation for trusting relationships. When early relationships are damaged, instead of secure attachments we can develop anxious, avoidant or disorganised attachments. We may then under-appreciate the importance of trusting attachments in sexual relationships and even though we may be well into adulthood, damaged relationships may affect future attachments. If people have put their trust in a sexual partner and that trust has been broken, it can lead to psychological damage. Like flesh wounds, these can heal but still leave scars. Trusting others becomes more difficult.

Reflection

I remember talking to a friend who had been divorced and was now happily remarried. Even so, he described the effect of his divorce on his life as like a book that had been soaked and dried out. The pages could be opened, but the damage to the print was unavoidable.

Another good friend from my university days was a serial monogamist. He tended to have relationships lasting several years but would then 'move on' to another long-term relationship. I remember him talking to me around his late thirties. He said that he was realising he would never be satisfied with a partner because he wanted someone with the intelligence of one former girlfriend, the looks of another, the sense of humour of a third, the values of yet another and so on. He recognised that this was an impossible expectation. The serial severed attachments had damaged his ability to see another partner as a whole person.

This culture of choice can lead to option fatigue. The fact that we can choose our sexual partners can actually cause anxiety that we will make a poor choice with the sense of failure that can ensue. Somehow, from an excess of choice, we can become oppressed by the very freedoms we crave.

Sexuality and gladness

So, what is this ideal healthy sexuality we should seek (even if we never quite attain it) in this life? The close relationship between our sexuality and our spirituality which courses through the veins of the Bible is described beautifully by Rob Bell in his book *Sex God* and reflects the call to us to exclusively worship the one true God by being faithful to one partner. It is refreshing to see the unabashed use of sexual relations as a metaphor for our relationship with God. The Old Testament is not prudish about sex. The Song of Songs is an explicit celebration of sexual relationships.

This mirrors psychological ideas around attachment- how strong attachments build our happiness and security, and how broken or distorted attachments make us vulnerable to depression. In loving relationships, power is given to the other, rendering us vulnerable to a broken heart. This power can be abused, or our powerlessness shared as an act of mutual trust and tenderness. Foster (1985) describes how our sexual commitment is best expressed in proportion to our life commitment to a potential partner to protect the other person and ourselves. In marriage liturgies, the vows of faithfulness - for better or for worse, for richer or for poorer, in sickness and in health - are a beautiful and poetic surrendering of our best interests to the interests of the other. What greater source of gladness could there be, and what better commitment to a healthy attachment can anyone aspire to? We all fail to meet these demands completely but endeavouring to meet them can be the finest journey.

Chapter 9

Understanding sin: combating resentment of God's love.

Then he said, 'There was once a man who had two sons. The younger said to his father, "Father, I want right now what's coming to me."

So the father divided the property between them. It wasn't long before the younger son packed his bags and left for a distant country. There, undisciplined and dissipated, he wasted everything he had. After he had gone through all his money, there was a bad famine all through that country and he began to hurt. He signed on with a citizen there who assigned him to his fields to slop the pigs. He was so hungry he would have eaten the corncobs in the pig slop, but no one would give him any.

That brought him to his senses. He said, "All those farmhands working for my father sit down to three meals a day, and here I am starving to death. I'm going back to my father. I'll say to him, Father, I've sinned against God, I've sinned before you; I don't deserve to be called your son. Take me on as a hired hand." He got right up and went home to his father.

"When he was still a long way off, his father saw him. His heart pounding, he ran out, embraced him, and kissed him. The son started his speech: "Father, I've sinned against God, I've sinned before you; I don't deserve to be called your son ever again."

But the father wasn't listening. He was calling to the servants, "Quick. Bring a clean set of clothes and dress him. Put the family ring on his finger and sandals on his feet. Then get a grain-fed heifer and roast it. We're going to feast! We're going to have a wonderful time! My son is here - given up for dead and now alive! Given up for lost and now found!" And they began to have a wonderful time.

All this time his older son was out in the field. When the day's work was done, he came in. As he approached the house, he heard the music and dancing. Calling over one of the houseboys, he asked what was going on. He told him, "Your brother came home. Your father has ordered a feast -barbecued beef! - because he has him home safe and sound."

The older brother stalked off in an angry sulk and refused to join in. His father came out and tried to talk to him, but he wouldn't listen. The son said, "Look how many years I've stayed here serving you, never giving you one moment of grief, but have you ever thrown a party for me and my friends? Then this son of yours who has thrown away your money on whores shows up and you go all out with a feast!"

His father said, "Son, you don't understand. You're with me all the time, and everything that is mine is yours—but this is a wonderful time, and we had to celebrate. This brother of yours was dead, and he's alive! He was lost, and he's found!"'

(Luke 15:11-32, MSG)

This parable which we so often call The Prodigal Son is one of three parables Jesus gave in response to a criticism from the Pharisees, the religiously committed people of his day, that he was hanging around with the wrong sort of people. The three parables were about how much God cares for 'lost' things- the sheep, the coin and then the son. In his meditation on this parable, Tim Keller calls the story, *The Prodigal God (2008)*, and reminds us that for the people who were expected to listen, the Pharisees, the character they were being compared to was the older son. Through this character we see that a source of spiritual depression for those committed to God can be a resentment of the generosity of God.

What was wrong with the older son? Firstly, it is noticeable that he was not looking for his brother, unlike the shepherd who went looking for the sheep or the woman searching high and low for the coin. He did not seem to love his father for his father's sake, but as a duty which he resented. Perhaps he loved him for his inheritance and realised that now his brother was back, that inheritance might halve. He resented his brother's repentance, perhaps believed it was superficial and manipulative. He resented his father's generosity in forgiving him- we can almost hear him railing, 'Silly old sentimental fool, can't he see through that fly-by-night, he'll never change'. He wanted his virtue to exclude his brother, not to express virtue in forgiving him.

Unless you are a remarkably spiritual person, you will have some recognition of the older son in yourself. That is why this is such a challenging and uncomfortable parable. Resentment of others can be such a powerful sin which grows like ivy around our hearts, strangling our joy in communing with others, hardening our hearts and depressing our spirit. It is a great source of sadness.

And, of course, there is a great example of this 'older-son resentment' in the Old Testament. Jonah is a prophet of God who is given a far-from-flattering portrait. After running away from God, his miraculous deliverance from certain drowning and his repentance, he delivers his message to the great city of Nineveh: 'Change your evil ways or be destroyed by the living God!' And what happens? Unlike so many prophets who are ignored, abused or killed by the chosen people of God in Israel, Jonah's message is heard! These pagans listen! They repent, and change. And Jonah can barely contain his disappointment. He despises God's willingness to forgive. He wants to see judgement. God, rather quietly, points out that to have mercy is more loving than to deliver rampant justice.

Virtue motivated by an advancement of our own status and excluding others is a source of spiritual depression. The Pharisees had a noble tradition and a strong faith. But their faith had become joyless, resentful of the forgiving love of God, wanting to exclude other people and express their own superiority. Our faith can become grasping and conditional. It is so easy to see faith as a deal with God: I live a good life; you make my life comfortable and easy. The corollary of this 'deal' is that if we see people we consider to be morally inferior being blessed in life, we resent them. This, indeed, is a human instinct that exists for people with no faith as well.

Reflection.

I will never forget a patient suffering from depression whom I assessed in clinic. She was a staunch atheist to the extent of being a member of a humanist society. Her daughter had tragically died in young adulthood from a medical condition. She said to me, 'I do not smoke, I do not drink, I have no god, and it's just not fair'.

Her construct of reality was that if she believed and did the 'right' things, bad things would not happen to her. She saw belief in God as a primitive weakness. But she still had a primal belief that if she did the right things, her life would avoid tragedy. She resented the shattering of this worldview. To her credit, I suggested she might read C.S. Lewis' meditation A Grief Observed, explaining it was a Christian book, and she went away and read it and found solace in the account of his suffering.

A very sincere and boldly active faith in God does not exempt us from 'older-son syndrome' either, however. I remember being in Leicester Square, London with a friend in my twenties and a Christian man was preaching to passers-by going to the cinema or theatre. We stopped to listen and he asked us if we were Christians. We told him we were. In response he asked my friend why he had an earring. He then started quoting the Old Testament arguing that adornment and jewellery was not of God. What struck me was that he was not glad that we shared his faith in God, but that he believed that he had a superior understanding of God. It struck me as sad that he could not metaphorically hug us, as the prodigal father did, but had to exclude us. I have been just as guilty, in my mind if not my behaviour (and probably both), as this gentleman on the London streets in the early 1990's.

I am convinced the greatest cure for this source of spiritual depression is a conviction of our sin. The idea of being convicted of our sin seems superficially to be depressing, and the world (and Satan in another of his great lies) tries to convince us of this. But conviction of our own sin is a great release in two ways. It makes us turn to base our faith on the grace of God and not our own efforts. Secondly, we identify with and accept all those who are seeking God and we become less judgemental and resentful of others. This has to be a 'spiritual treatment' for this source of spiritual depression. Christians can easily overestimate their own virtue.

John Cassian, a third century monk, spoke of a sadness that can be a source of joy, and this is a sadness about our own faults. This sadness brings us joy because it can lead to change in ourselves and greater patience with, and acceptance of, others (Jamison, 2008).

We need to be wary that we do not become weary of well-doing, especially in the 'middle age' of our spiritual journey when the Christian life may lose its novelty and freshness. This is as true for our spiritual lives as for our careers and our marriages; we have to work at keeping them fresh.

We can become reliant on our activities as the mainstay of our spiritual lives, and then resent believers whom we perceive as less active than ourselves. As one very wise person stated, the biggest threat to our devotional lives is service. We need to stop, reflect, contemplate, meditate and pray about our inner attitudes, our faith, our understanding of God. It may be wise to take time out with a spiritual advisor or mentor to reflect on our spiritual lives.

We need to be vigilant in noticing our resentments. We can so easily let our inner criticism of others and gossip between each other erode our relationships. Paul frequently calls us to build each other up, and we need to put this into practice.
We need to look for the good in others and not for their faults and shortcomings. To be an encouragement to others is a spiritual gift we all need to nurture. Barnabas was the son of encouragement and we need to emulate him. He was willing to rehabilitate Mark despite Mark's mistakes. In actively encouraging others we enrich our own spirit as well as theirs. After all, the author of the letter to the Hebrews (10: 4-25) says that the purpose of gathering together as a church is to encourage each other: to 'spur one another on to love and good deeds', the wonderful corollary of which is that we will inevitably be spurred on ourselves.

Chapter 10

Understanding how we relate: combating the scapegoating of others.

Adam slept with Eve his wife. She conceived and had Cain. She said, 'I've gotten a man, with God's help!' Then she had another baby, Abel. Abel was a herdsman and Cain a farmer.

Time passed. Cain brought an offering to God from the produce of his farm. Abel also brought an offering, but from the firstborn animals of his herd, choice cuts of meat. God liked Abel and his offering, but Cain and his offering didn't get his approval. Cain lost his temper and went into a sulk.

God spoke to Cain: 'Why this tantrum? Why the sulking? If you do well, won't you be accepted? And if you don't do well, sin is lying in wait for you, ready to pounce; it's out to get you, you've got to master it.'

Cain had words with his brother. They were out in the field; Cain came at Abel his brother and killed him.

God said to Cain, 'Where is Abel your brother?' He said, 'How should I know? Am I his babysitter?' God said, 'What have you done! The voice of your brother's blood is calling to me from the ground. From now on you'll get nothing but curses from this ground; you'll be driven from this ground that has opened its arms to receive the blood of your murdered brother. You'll farm this ground, but it will no longer give you its best. You'll be a homeless wanderer on Earth.'

Cain said to God, 'My punishment is too much. I can't take it! You've thrown me off the land and I can never again face you. I'm a homeless wanderer on Earth and whoever finds me will kill me.'

God told him, 'No. Anyone who kills Cain will pay for it seven times over.' God put a mark on Cain to protect him so that no one who met him would kill him.

Cain left the presence of God and lived in No-Man's-Land, east of Eden. (Genesis 4: 1-16, MSG)

We can view our lives as a personal-internal world and also from a relational-social perspective. This is evident in theology as individual relationships with God are emphasised in some traditions and God's relationship with whole communities - the Hebrew tribes in the Old Testament and the church of the New Testament - in others. In psychiatry we talk of an individualistic biological psychiatry - where genes and neurophysiology may determine our mental health - and social psychiatry where interactions with others impact on the aetiology of mental illness. We tend to be very individualistic in western culture compared to most cultures, but still recognise how our relationships influence our wellbeing.

The story of Cain and Abel has profound insights into how we relate to each other.

Rene Girard is a literary critic, social scientist and Catholic theologian. He has developed an understanding of how we relate that casts a new understanding not just on this story of Cain and Abel, but also on Job, the suffering servant of Isaiah and ultimately the passion, death and resurrection of Jesus Christ. This has been called mimetic theory (Allison, 1997; Kirwan, 2004).

Mimetic theory can be summarised in three stages. The first is that our desires are determined by following the desires of another person or persons whom we wish to emulate. Initially this leads to a positive relationship between the person wishing to follow and the person being followed. The second stage is that conflict and rivalry grow between the follower and the followed. This is usually painful for both parties. The third stage is that we deal with the tension of conflict between the follower and the followed by finding a third person or group to blame for the conflict and we scapegoat this person. We can inflict violence on the scapegoat, either by excluding them or even committing actual violence to them.

The metaphor of the scapegoat is biblical from the book of Leviticus, when the Hebrews placed the sin of the people on two goats: one is sacrificed, the other released to wander in the wilderness. A modern definition is, 'a person who is blamed for the wrongdoings or mistakes of others' (Concise Oxford English Dictionary).

An obvious example from history is anti-Semitism. In Germany in the 1930s, there was economic depression and social chaos. A coherent and sophisticated society was struggling to understand why it was suffering so much. In turning on the Jewish community, and blaming this sector of society, the people of Germany could express the frustration and sense of humiliation they felt after the first world war. The subsequent violence remains one of the most shocking episodes in history, perpetrated in a nation which was the most intellectually precocious in the world at the time, whose scientists, doctors, philosophers and theologians were international leaders. One reason this period of history still holds a morbid fascination is the struggle to understand how this most advanced nation could descend to such barbarity so quickly.

Less obvious examples can be found within families and churches. Church communities are made up of people like you and me - flawed, sinful, of different theological persuasions. If groups are united by a belief system, tensions will still develop within the group. How easy it is to manage these tensions by externalising the blame. The pastor is not good enough, too liberal, too fundamental, does not evangelise, has no depth to his teaching, too traditional, too quick to adopt new things. Or we might blame another group in the church community, who do not want charismatic gifts expressed, or are too keen on charismatic gifts. How easy it is to exclude others, or to exclude ourselves, by splitting off and forming a new church or even a new denomination. But this schism is a slippery slope to constant schisms, as tensions re-emerge and new reasons need to be found, with new expulsions or splits.

In families, tensions between spouses can be blamed on in-laws. The most painful is when marital tension is blamed on children. One of the most distressing experiences as a psychiatrist is treating patients who were scapegoated as children by adults frustrated at their own lives. Nothing seems to be as devastating to our developing mental wellbeing as being told we are useless, stupid, will come to nothing by a parent who feels this about themselves or their marriage but finds it easier to take it out on their children than be honest with themselves. All parents have power and can use it for good or ill.

Tragically even the Church has been guilty of emotionally abusing children in institutions in this way. Children of unmarried mothers were scandalously treated as inferior in institutions and in society as a whole. We cannot pretend this is not true or we risk finding other scapegoats. Another common example is a parent who struggles as their child becomes independent and no longer wishes to follow shared desires. Rather than deal with this tension in the relationship, the spouse of the child can be blamed for 'taking away' the son or daughter, leading to chronic disharmony and dishonesty. Likewise adult offspring, in facing the flaws in their personalities, can exaggerate the responsibility of their parents and scapegoat them instead of addressing their own need for change.

Reflection

Recently, in a British hospital, standards fell drastically and it is estimated 1200 lives were lost that would not have been lost if standards had been equivalent to other hospitals. A woman whose mother died at the hospital in distressing circumstances started a campaign against the unacceptable care. Official enquiries vindicated her campaign, and the hospital was put under special measures. Subsequently standards of care improved.

Because of a threat of closure of their hospital, this woman was subject to a hate campaign by local people. She received death threats and her mother's grave was desecrated. Finally, she had to leave her hometown because of the hate she was experiencing.

Some people took the risk of their hospital closing, which was due to inadequate care, and blamed the person who had exposed the inadequate care (which actually led to a rapid improvement in the hospital's performance).

The book of Job exposes a very subtle form of scapegoating that still occurs- the scapegoating of those who suffer. Job is afflicted by many troubles- the loss of his wealth, his children and finally his health. Job's 'comforters' have a decided opinion - the person who suffers has brought it on themselves through their wrongdoing. They wrap this up in a theology of a just God. The fascinating thing about the story of Job is that we know this is not true from the beginning - it is Satan who has done this with the permission of God because Job is a good man! But it is Job's friends who use theological arguments, whilst Job simply rails against God, saying that this is just not fair. And God justifies Job and condemns the friends.

Is one of the many messages in the book of Job that we are easily tempted to make sense of the suffering of others (which unnerves us as we know it could happen to ourselves) by adopting the opinion that they have brought it on themselves? Refugees have not attended to the welfare of their nation. People have smoked, drunk too much alcohol or taken drugs in the past. They have not taken exercise and have been overweight. They have been lazy and not been willing to work. They were not good enough parents. Scapegoating suffering is particularly condemned in scripture. We should identify the sick, the prisoner and the naked as Christ himself.

Reflection

As a doctor, I have noticed how easy it is to scapegoat a patient who is not getting better. It is easy to fall back on an argument that the patient is not trying hard enough to change their lifestyle or engage in therapy. This is probably out of fear of being scapegoated ourselves, because patients can indeed scapegoat their doctors. I noticed when my wife was receiving care for her cancer, I almost became sick with anxiety as the consultant walked into the room. Such a reaction must be a heavy burden for an oncologist to be under, over and over again. When treatment stops working it is easy to scapegoat a clinician for not spotting the cancer earlier. To live with the pain of the situation without scapegoating and blaming can feel too much to bear.

It is fascinating that in the first chapters of Genesis, such deep spiritual, theological and psychological truths are described. Cain has been in conflict with God. His offering is not acceptable. It is not even made clear what is inadequate about his offering. It is intriguing that God warns him that sin can take him over, he needs to master it. But Cain does not listen. Instead of meditating on his conflict with God, he turns his negative feelings onto a third party - his innocent brother Abel, who has nothing to do with that conflict. It results in violence and murder. But God is clear that he sides with the victim, with Abel, and will not ignore the scapegoating and subsequent violence.

This sets a pattern. God does not ignore the scapegoating of and violence towards the Hebrew slaves in Egypt. He will not tolerate the scapegoating of Job by his accusing friends but will vindicate him. He will promise a suffering servant who will take the sins of the world on to himself. And in the final act of identification with the victim, God will send his own Son, who will remain sinless, but be scapegoated not just by religious leaders and powerful soldiers, but by all of fallen creation as God will die on a cross: the innocent victim again being scapegoated for the sins of others. But this time there will be a breaking of the fallen way of things, as the victim of scapegoating violence breaks the hold and horror of death.

We must not be fooled. We are like Cain. We can find our conflicts with others unbearable, especially with those we admire and seek to emulate. When we are in this situation we can seek to unite with our admired group through scapegoating others. This may work in the short term, but never works over time as the tensions return, and by then we have the additional burden of unjustified violence against the innocent scapegoat. We have called out 'Crucify him', said, 'It is better for one man to die than that the whole people perish', driven the nails in deeper.

This is a great source of spiritual depression. When we are struggling with our own inadequacies, our own sin, or in our relationships with those we admire and wish to emulate, we need to contemplate these situations with honesty, humility and prayer. We must be very wary if we begin to scapegoat another person, another group when we are anxious and depressed. We may not kill, we may not take part in a holocaust, but gossip, family schisms, bitterness and church divisions are frequently caused by such dynamics. Time spent with spiritual counsellors, directors, mentors or friends exploring our darker thoughts can strip us of our tendency to scapegoat.

Chapter 11

Understanding brutality: combating despair at inflicted suffering.

But this time the man wasn't willing to spend another night. He got things ready, left, and went as far as Jebus (Jerusalem) with his pair of saddled donkeys, his concubine, and his servant. At Jebus, though, the day was nearly gone. The servant said to his master, 'It's late; let's go into this Jebusite city and spend the night.'

But his master said, 'We're not going into any city of foreigners. We'll go on to Gibeah.' He directed his servant, 'Keep going. Let's go on ahead. We'll spend the night either at Gibeah or Ramah.'

So, they kept going. As they pressed on, the sun finally left them in the vicinity of Gibeah, which belongs to Benjamin. They left the road there to spend the night at Gibeah.

The Levite went and sat down in the town square, but no one invited them in to spend the night. Then, late in the evening, an old man came in from his day's work in the fields. He was from the hill country of Ephraim and lived temporarily in Gibeah where all the local citizens were Benjaminites. When the old man looked up and saw the traveller in the town square, he said, 'Where are you going? And where are you from?'

The Levite said, 'We're just passing through. We're coming from Bethlehem on our way to a remote spot in the hills of Ephraim. I come from there. I've just made a trip to Bethlehem in Judah and I'm on my way back home, but no one has invited us in for the night. We wouldn't be any trouble: We have food and straw for the donkeys, and bread and wine for the woman, the young man, and me—we don't need anything.'

The old man said, 'It's going to be all right; I'll take care of you. You aren't going to spend the night in the town square.' He took them home and fed the donkeys. They washed up and sat down to a good meal.

They were relaxed and enjoying themselves when the men of the city, a gang of local hell-raisers all, surrounded the house and started pounding on the door. They yelled for the owner of the house, the old man, 'Bring out the man who came to your house. We want to have sex with him.'

He went out and told them, 'No, brothers! Don't be obscene—this man is my guest. Don't commit this outrage. Look, my virgin daughter and his concubine are here. I'll bring them out for you. Abuse them if you must, but don't do anything so senselessly vile to this man.'

But the men wouldn't listen to him. Finally, the Levite pushed his concubine out the door to them. They raped her repeatedly all night long. Just before dawn they let her go. The woman came back and fell at the door of the house where her master was sleeping. When the sun rose, there she was.

It was morning. Her master got up and opened the door to continue his journey. There she was, his concubine, crumpled in a heap at the door, her hands on the threshold.

'Get up,' he said. 'Let's get going.' There was no answer.

He lifted her onto his donkey and set out for home. When he got home, he took a knife and dismembered his concubine—cut her into twelve pieces. He sent her, piece by piece, throughout the country of Israel. And he ordered the men he sent out, 'Say to every man in Israel: "Has such a thing as this ever happened from the time the Israelites came up from the land of Egypt until now? Think about it! Talk it over. Do something!"'

(Judges 19, MSG).

This is one of the most disturbing stories in the Bible, but closely resembles another. The account of the destruction of Sodom and Gomorrah in Genesis is better known. The angels of God visit Sodom and Gomorrah knowing of its depravity. Lot meets them and anxiously persuades them to stay at his home. A mob turn up and demand to gang rape them. As a result, these cities are destroyed. The story represents how the people of Canaan were brutal and depraved.

Several centuries follow. God has kept his covenant with Abraham to choose the Hebrew people. They spend centuries in Egypt, becoming numerous but enslaved. God delivers them miraculously from slavery. He appears to Moses and gives a Law that is to define them as a people, and guide them as to how to live, setting an example for all peoples and times. Despite failures as well as successes, they settle in Canaan.

And then this story. A Hebrew man avoids the Canaanite city and trusts his fellow Hebrews at Gibeah. And practically the same things happen as happened in Sodom and Gomorrah, only worse, as the concubine, who seems to be the only person in this story whose behaviour is not brutal, is gang raped and dies. The Hebrew people have declined into the depravity and brutality of Sodom and Gomorrah despite the incredible revelation of God. A civil war is the result.

Is this relevant for the modern world?

Many people think the Old Testament is primitive and barbaric, irrelevant for understanding the modern world. They could not be more wrong. The Old Testament addresses the most fundamental aspects of human nature in an honest and direct way. In some ways it is primitive, in that it addresses the prime aspects of our characters. But these kind of episodes - are they relevant now?

Most of us know they are when we read or watch the news. In Rwanda 800,000 people were killed by their neighbours in a matter of weeks in 1994. In the resulting war in central Africa, rape of women became commonplace by different militias and armies. In Afghanistan and Pakistan women have acid thrown in their faces for the most minor of so-called misdemeanours - sometimes by their own parents. In living memory, 6 million people were killed in a systematic, industrial manner for being Jewish. I remember a psychiatric conference in 1995 I attended where I heard a talk from an elderly lady. During the 1940s she had been in a psychiatric institution where almost all the other patients had been killed in gas chambers with the collusion of psychiatrists because they had a mental illness. She had been spared because she was good at cleaning the hospital floors.

But surely these things are remote from our civilised western democracies? I have worked in a rural British county for the last 20 years. It is a lovely place to live, with low crime rates. However, I have personally treated patients who were repeatedly raped by their fathers from as young an age as 2 years old. Unfortunately, this is not rare anywhere in the UK - ask any mental health clinician working in the UK National Health Service. One child is killed by adults each week in the UK. We often scapegoat social services for child deaths, but violence and abuse of children in Britain is endemic. Rates are higher in parts of the US. Domestic abuse of women is also endemic in our societies, often of a sadistic nature. Women's refuges are needed in all counties of England. A woman is killed by a man every three days. Whilst some truly horrific homicides make press headlines, most do not, such is the tragically unsurprising nature of violence against women by men.

So, the understanding of the brutality of men (and sometimes of women) is not a remote, archaic Old Testament irrelevance.

It is an urgent description of human behaviour. This is about not burying our heads in the sand. And God will not us let us bury our heads in the sand if we take the trouble to read and learn from the Old Testament.

A running theme throughout the Old Testament is to protect and care for the widows, orphans and aliens (foreigners). In that time, these people were desperately vulnerable to abuse and exploitation. This was a radical call from God to protect the weak. God calls us to 'act justly, love mercy and walk humbly' (Micah 6:8) - the true shalom of God.

Sometimes I do despair of human behaviour and it does make me feel low. When God decides to destroy human beings in the story of Noah, I can understand why.

Reflection

I have honestly hoped for the death of one patient's father. I am not saying that is right, but it is true that I did so. When I discussed that with the rest of my colleagues in the mental health team, others also had similar feelings, even fantasising about hiring someone to kill him.

<u>Christians and the church can be like Gibeah</u>

But we must remember that we are capable of similar brutality. We may refrain from the more severe forms of abuse, but we can be tyrannical and brutal in other ways, especially in the privacy of our own homes. And just as Hebrew society had descended to the levels of brutality seen in Sodom and Gomorrah, modern Christian institutions can be tyrannical and brutal if we do not keep close to God, just as the Hebrew town of Gibeah was. The past institutional abuse of children in the Roman Catholic churches demonstrates this. Recent disclosures in Australia have revealed that in certain Roman Catholic institutions forty per cent of members have been accused of child sexual abuse, suggesting an institutional level of collusion and tolerance of depravity. However, the abuse of children is not confined to the Catholic Church. A recent report from the Independent Inquiry into Child Sexual Abuse (IICSA) in the UK in 2021 reports abuse of children across many religious institutions including the Church of England, all denominations of Christianity and in Islamic and Jewish communities. Non-religious esteemed organisations have also harboured abusers of the vulnerable, including the NHS, the BBC and football clubs.

<u>How can we make amends?</u>

We are called to fight evil. It is part of our calling to advocate for the weak in society and protect them from those of us who abuse our power- and that includes all of us. We need to support structures and institutions which seek to do this. We can make fun of institutional structures such as safeguarding and health and safety, but these movements genuinely fight the evils of abuse and negligence and we should fight for them. To combat spiritual depression, we must fight evil.

We must realise that without God we drift towards brutality, as individuals and as societies. This is not to say people who are not Christians all do so, that is plainly untrue. And, sadly, the Christian church has always been sinful enough to be brutal itself. Christians need to be reflective and vigilant to avoid brutality. But as people forget God, the Christian values underpinning our law and institutions drift away from the law of God which emphasises that all people are made in the image of God and therefore are sacred, and society can become brutalised. Declaring the truth of the Christian message is not just about calling individuals to follow Christ, but for our lives, in society, to be transformed. Salvation is not completed at conversion; it is a lifelong and ongoing process of healing.

Richard Rohr in *The world, the Flesh and the Devil* expresses the view that evil is often an act perpetrated collectively by institutions rather than individuals. Jesus often condemns groups rather than individuals, such as whole towns (Jerusalem, Chorazim) and authority groups (Pharisees, chief priests, moneylenders). We need to examine how we function in institutions such as churches, universities, private companies, public bodies like the NHS, and hold them to account for their actions. It is easy to hide behind the institution to avoid responsibility, but we make up the institutions. We must fight evil in our personal lives and our collective lives.

Chapter 12

Being glad: nurturing joy.

But the fruit of the Spirit is love, joy, peace, forbearance, kindness, goodness, faithfulness, gentleness and self-control.

(Galatians 5:22 NIV)

Rejoice always, pray continually, give thanks in all circumstances; for this is God's will for you in Christ Jesus.

(1 Thessalonians 5:16-18, NIV).

Consider it pure joy, my brothers and sisters, whenever you face trials of many kinds, because you know that the testing of your faith produces perseverance.

(James 1:2-3, NIV)

But rejoice inasmuch as you participate in the sufferings of Christ, so that you may be overjoyed when his glory is revealed.

(1 Peter 4:13, NIV)

Rejoice in the Lord always. I will say it again: Rejoice!

(Phil 4.4 NIV)

I know what it is to be in need, and I know what it is to have plenty. I have learned the secret of being content in any and every situation, whether well fed or hungry, whether living in plenty or in want.

(Phil 4: 12 NIV)

Godliness with contentment is great gain.

(1 Timothy 6:6 NIV)

As I have already said, my natural state is one of slight melancholy. I am not that comfortable being joyful. I really enjoy contemplating and discussing the complexities of a meaningful life. Sitting in a pub discussing these things with a friend is one of my life's deepest pleasures. People have told me at times that I am a bit intense and can be contrary, and I always think, 'What's wrong with that! I enjoy being intense and I enjoy debating with people!' I think there are some good sides to this - I have really enjoyed my work as a psychiatrist because of the endless uncertainties and debates, which I know other doctors find frustrating and even tortuous! I also enjoy the uncertainties and diverse opinions in Christian belief, whereas others want certainty and clarity. I am going off on a tangent- another source of joy for me and frustration for others! The New Testament writers are very clear that being joyful is not only desirable but necessary for our welfare and a product of the work of God in our lives.

The English word joy is defined as a state of happiness and pleasure. The origin is from the Latin word *gaudier* meaning rejoice and we also have the words enjoyment and gaudy from the same source. From the Greek *redone*, meaning pleasure, we get the words hedonism, the pursuit of pleasure, and the psychiatric word anhedonia. This latter term is the inability to enjoy what we normally enjoy and a core symptom of depression.

It is interesting that joy has a slightly spiritual air, seems purer, whereas hedonism is seen as a more bodily, base pleasure: part of the platonic split between body, mind and spirit which has polluted Christianity and medicine - in the latter, viewed through this paradigm, diseases of the body and mind are split in an unhealthy way.

As the biblical Judaeo-Christian teaching is holistic and does not separate body, mind and spirit, we can assume that the pleasures of the body are as worthy and God-inspired as the pleasures of the mind and spirit. However just as the pleasures of the body can become self-serving and corrupted, so can the pleasures of the mind and spirit. Asceticism can be a proud self-serving declaration of our spiritual prowess just as hedonism can be a proud, self-serving declaration of our physical prowess. But physical pleasures are still pleasures,

God created, to be sought and celebrated, to be lived and loved.

Christian teaching calls us, commands us even, to rejoice, express joy, express happiness and pleasure. We are also called to share in the sufferings of the world as Christ did.

John the baptiser was accused of being an ascetic for his abstinence in food and clothing, whereas Jesus was accused of being a hedonist. Accusatory eyes saw Jesus as associating with prostitutes and dodgy people, joining them in their eating and drinking. It is striking that Christ's first miracle was turning water into wine at a party - after the guests had drunk all that was provided!

Some people believe life is about hard work and endurance. (These are good things, but not the only good things.) They can become inherently suspicious of people who seem to be enjoying life. They can interpret this as superficial, not taking life seriously or being lazy. An over-emphasis on a work ethic can lead to an inability to simply enjoy the pleasures in life, or a feeling of guilt in doing so. I confess I have been guilty of these tendencies and have to 'work' at simply stopping and being joyful in the pleasures of existence. When Jesus taught his disciples to be like little children, maybe that childlike sense of wonder, ability to be absorbed in play and to be utterly in the moment was one aspect he was emphasising.

So how on earth are we supposed to rejoice in the Lord always? How are we to live in a state of happiness and pleasure? Is being morose a sin? How can we seek pleasure in a good way?

Jeremy Jernigan, in his book *Redeeming Pleasure; how our pursuit of pleasure mirrors our hunger for God*, describes quite rightly how our desire for pleasure is an inherent part of being human, how we are created by God. The problems arise when we pursue pleasure on our terms, which results in us experiencing less of it. A Christian hedonism[7] is a noble goal - the pursuit of pleasures as they were designed to be experienced by the being who created them. Indeed, fundamentally, we are called to pursue God purely for the

[7] The author has become aware that this expression is used extensively by John Piper in his writings (Piper, J. (2011). Desiring god: Meditations of a Christian hedonist. Multnomah Pub) but he has always used it himself to describe the enjoyment of God-given pleasures for themselves as gifts from God.

pleasure of doing so. God does not need our love or company, he enjoys it. Desire is created by God. As C.S. Lewis writes in his sermon *The Weight of Glory* (1996)

> *If there lurks in most modern minds the notion that to desire our own good and earnestly to hope for the enjoyment of it is a bad thing, I submit that this notion has crept in from Kant and the Stoics and is no part of the Christian faith* (p. 25-26).

Love and community

We can note from the above biblical passages that:

Paul commands us to rejoice and be joyful as a Christian responsibility.

Joy is a product of the work of the Holy Spirit in us - as a fruit, a natural part of our growth if we are immersed in God.

We are specifically called to be joyful when we are suffering or under some kind of trial or persecution, and to be thankful in all circumstances.

Fundamentally I think a key is grounding our happiness and pleasure in love, because then it is not narcissistic, proud or self-glorifying, but connects our happiness and pleasure with God and other fellow human beings. The obvious example is our sexual pleasure being grounded in the committed love towards another and not solely in our own (God created) desires with less regard to the other person. We are called to community - our sexual pleasure is not individualistic but needs to be mutual. But this applies to our mental and spiritual pleasures as well - wanting to share in discussions that enrich all participants, not just win the argument. Wanting to be part of a church community that serves all, not just ourselves. If we approach church as solely a meeting of our needs, we will always be frustrated.

This is why community is so important. Being focussed on ourselves can be important at times but can lead to a destructive narcissism, a destructive self-loathing or simple loneliness. I was talking to a pastor friend about what is core to being Christian. He used to think it was individualistic, our 'personal relationship with God', but has changed his mind. He feels gathering together is more important because it is being the community of God, which is harder work, more sacrificial and more creative. I would agree with this.

I have worked in the British National Health Service for over 30 years and been part of various churches for longer and there is a similarity. When you do your own thing in both, it generally achieves relatively little, but when you work in a team or in a community you can achieve so much more, even change the world. That is because I am good at some things and not others. Some of my work is in research and when a group of people get together with different strengths, wow, things really start to happen. The recent *Recovery Trial* during the COVID-19 pandemic is a case in point. By September 2020 a broad coalition of academics, the NHS research network and doctors and nurses treating desperately ill patients delivered a complex trial in three months demonstrating dexamethasone, a relatively cheap steroid, was effective in reducing the death rate from this awful disease. By April 2020 this simple treatment had saved 20,000 lives in the UK and 650,000 lives world-wide. Covid-19 vaccine development and research were remarkably rapid across the world needing the collaboration of different teams and skills. In the UK alone by September 2021 vaccines were estimated to have prevented 24 million infections and saved 120,000 lives. COVID-19 has been a terrible illness but led to remarkable advances in team coordination in health research. The challenge now, at the time of writing, is to share these advances with poorer nations where vaccination rates are much lower.

It is the same with church. None of us are good at everything. Some are good teachers, some good organisers, some great pastorally with the struggling and others just good at supporting and encouraging those doing the work. When a 'spiritual team' gets things together- we can change the world! We have seen recent examples- Amnesty International set up in the 1960s, foodbanks in the UK in the 2010s, the 24/7 prayer movement in the 'noughties', the Jubilee campaign to eliminate developing world debt at the turn of the century. The joy in these and much smaller achievements is significant and is born in loving communities doing things together, which individually we cannot do.

In some ways a loving community, which is the ideal of church, is like a healthy soil. It is full of messy diversity in which ideas can fall like a seed and grow. Good soil is full of different lifeforms. Each individually is pretty insignificant but together is the source of all life and allows life to germinate and flourish. If we suppress some of those lifeforms with insecticide and pesticide the soil degenerates. To be a little narcissistic (a small amount of narcissism is actually quite healthy as Jeremy Holmes observes!) when writing this book I had a few ideas, but they grew massively in discussing them with my community. There is no greater joy than ideas forming and germinating in a loving community. The origin of universities - those great incubators of ideas – was in monasteries: loving Christian communities.

Gratitude

Joy is a state of mind that can make us resilient to despair because we share in mutual pleasure with others and with God and this binds us together, we are not isolated. And joy in the pleasures of this world makes us thankful. Gratitude must be one of the most powerful of antidepressants, and there is evidence of this in psychiatric research (Kendler 2003). If we seek the pleasures of this world grounded in love, we become grateful to God and expressing this gratitude elevates us from our suffering. Gratitude is often about taking time to notice - to notice the good things in our lives. I remember as a teenager finding nothing more annoying that people telling me to count by blessings, but with maturity this old cliche is obviously therapeutic. When I am stressed or feeling down, going for a short walk and taking in the beauty of the natural world, thanking God for it, nearly always helps my troubled mind. At other times phoning a good friend and just feeling thankful for them can lift me out of negative thought patterns about myself or other people. The act of thanking someone lifts my spirit, and if someone thanks me for something, I am often on cloud nine.

Reflection

I remember being at a national psychiatric conference a few years ago. A person I did not recognise came up to me and told me that when she was a medical student, about twenty years earlier, she had been on a placement with me for a few weeks when I was a junior doctor in East London. We had driven around Bow and Poplar in my Morris Minor seeing patients in the community and she enjoyed it so much she had trained in psychiatry and was working in south London. She wanted to thank me. I was on cloud nine, and still am five years later, because her encouragement gave me so much joy.

Creativity

We can also return to the very beginning of the Bible to get to a radical source of our joy. In the act of creation, there is a joy, almost playfulness, in the description of God's behaviour. And we are called to partake in this ongoing act of creation. Just as there is joy in the new birth of a child, it seems most basic creative deeds can produce joy, from cooking to gardening, writing books to decorating the house, painting a masterpiece to drawing cartoons.

Reflection

My daughter, when she was ten years old, took to writing and drawing her own comics, and spent hours doing so, modelling her characters on Dennis the Menace. I was struck by the joy she had in these acts of creation.

There is a multitude of research projects showing that creative activities, especially work, is good for our mental health and builds resilience to depression. We are the image of God - we are born to create and be a co-worker with God. A major finding over the last 50 years in psychiatry is the importance of occupation and work for our mental health. For patients suffering from psychosis, support back into employment has been shown to be of immense benefit to people. Homeless charities have job creation at the heart of their holistic programmes. A fulfilling job and career are immense sources of joy. The negative stereotype of employment as drudgery, perhaps a consequence of the dehumanising nature of some factory work after industrialisation, needs to be replaced with the hope that work can be a source of joy, creativity and wonder.

And indeed, God is the source of our joy because God is joyful. 'The joy of the Lord is your strength' (Nehemiah 8:10). Jesus said, 'I told you this so that my joy may be in you and that your joy may be complete' (John 15:11). We do not worship a morose God- we worship a joyful, joy-full, God (Gillespie, 2013). Indeed, where God is, there will be joy, and to deny ourselves joy is to exclude God in our lives. This is the danger of asceticism - if self-denial has no higher purpose, it is narcissistic and excludes God.

Contentment

Martyn Lloyd-Jones described a 'final cure' to spiritual depression. In the book of Philippians, Paul describes himself as 'sufficient' whatever his circumstances, whether in plenty or in want. It is this sufficiency in God that will keep us joyful, because we are not dependent on our circumstances. If we seek to be joyful by practicing the presence of God, we will not be dependent on our status, our relationships, our church, our wealth, our health, our intellect, our looks or anything else. We may enjoy all of these as God given blessings, but our state of being should be the same with or without them. If we end our days incapable and witless, it will make no difference, because our joy is in the God who is there and loves us unconditionally. And the Christian life is an activity - an activity of God within us. He can transform us to live in this sufficiency in him - indeed that is what we are called to do: to let God do his work in us.

So, whatever is happening in our lives, let us seek to be thankful and to notice the pleasures we are given from God. We are called to be joyful, not in a fake denial of our suffering, but in a balanced and realistic assessment of the great gifts of this life and the great hope we have in the resurrection of Christ, the new heaven and the new earth.

The future, after all, is good.

Ideas for personal reflection and small group discussion

Chapter 1: Spiritual depression

- What is your temperament? How do you allow for these tendencies to have their place but not overwhelm your thinking and behaviour?
- What are your strengths? Have your strengths ever led you into making mistakes?
- Have you got the balance right between self-examination and morbid introspection?

Chapter 2: The grace of God

- Consider the last setback or disappointment in your life. What was your immediate view on why it had happened? Did you think that God was punishing you in any way? What about now- how do you feel the setback fits in with your beliefs about God?
- Adam and Eve struggled to stand naked before God. How are you at being exposed before God? How do you feel God would react?
- Think of the person in this world you struggle with most. Now consider that God loves them unconditionally. How does this affect your view of them?

Chapter 3: The invisibility of God

- What do you do in your solitude? What positive and negative feelings do you have about what you do in your solitude?
- When did you last feel ignored or unnoticed? How do you feel about that now?
- Who do you spiritually admire in your community who often goes unnoticed?

Chapter 4: Spiritual narcissism

- Reflect on your past fantasies on how your spiritual life might develop. What has come to pass and what has not?

If those hopes had come true, would that have been a good thing?

- What dreams for yourself do you have that are healthy if fulfilled or unhealthy if fulfilled?
- What is your relationship with doubt?
- How have you been disappointed in your own life and disappointed with others? What does that say about your expectations of yourself and of the other?
- Have you considered your own death? What do you fear and why?

Chapter 5: Repentance and forgiveness

- Reflect on the last time you felt exposed at doing something wrong. How would have you felt if you had not been exposed?
- How do you feel about the idea of confessing your sins to another? If you were to do this, who would it be with?
- Is there anyone in your life who you find it difficult to forgive? How might you deal with this?
- Is there anything in your life for which you find it difficult to forgive yourself?
- Is there anything you feel guilty about which is not justified? How can you be helped with this false guilt?

Chapter 6: Clearing our minds

- Are struggling with angry imaginative conversations with anyone particular at the moment?
- Are you anxious about anything in the future at the moment that you cannot do something about today? How can you let go of that unfruitful worry?

Chapter 7: Combatting the desire for more.

- Do you feel you have enough money, friends, status and influence? If the honest answer is no, how much would be enough?
- What is the most likely source of desire for you: money, friends, status, influence or something else?

Chapter 8: Being sexual.

- Have you had damaging experiences in the past in sexual relationships? How has that affected your ability to trust people?
- How do you feel you are able to trust people in a close relationship? Secure, anxious, avoidant, disorganised- are these words descriptive of how you can be in relationships?
- How can we persuade young people that sexual restraint can be a source of joy?

Chapter 9: Combating resentment.

- Who was the last person you resented and why?
- When did you last feel resented? Why do you think that person resented you?
- In which situations are you most prone to resenting others?
- Consider if you resent God for forgiving any person, in the Bible, in history or in your experience.

Chapter 10: Scapegoating

- Who did you last scapegoat?
- Who are you prone to scapegoat most? A spouse, a relative, a boss, a colleague, the government, an authority figure?
- Have you ever scapegoated anyone for your frustrations with church?

Chapter 11: Brutality

- When have you felt despair at the news? Does this affect your theology or ideas about God?
- How do you feel you can fight evil, individually and as part of a community?

Chapter 12: Joy

- Have you ever felt guilty for enjoying life? How do you understand that now?
- What gives you most joy at the moment?
- How are you able to be creative at the moment?

- What are your strengths and weaknesses when working creatively in a community? What do you lack that you need from others?
- What are you particularly thankful for at this point in your life?
- How has work enriched your life?
- Where do you think your contentment (or lack of it) comes from?

Acknowledgements

I would like to thank Dee Molton and Susan Bennett for help with editing this book.

I had great help from friends who read and gave me feedback: Penny Shutt, Tracy and Jesse Foot, Josiah Gillespie, Lyndsey Clarke, Sheila Lile, Hazel Cartlidge Klaus, Joan Whittaker, Matt and Louise Frost, Gaz Daly, Jacqueline and Jeremy Mould, Ben Basterfield, Jane Laugharne, Chris Mould, John Reed, Hugh Nelson and Rohit Shankar.

Andrew Bisgrove created the cover art work.

References

Allison, J (1997). *Living in the End Times.* SPCK, London.

Bell, R. (2008). *The Gods Aren't Angry.* (DVD) HarperChristian Resources.

Bell, R. (2007). *Sex God.* Zondervan, Grand Rapids, Michigan.

Bell, R. (2006). *Nooma: Breathe.* Zondervan, Grand Rapids, Michigan.

Comer, J. M. (2019). *The Ruthless Elimination of Hurry: How to Stay Emotionally Healthy and Spiritually Alive in the Chaos of the Modern World.* WaterBrook Press, Colorado.

Dawkins, R. (2006). *The God Delusion.* Bantam Books, New York.

Ellis, A. (1980). *Psychotherapy and atheistic values.* Journal of Consulting and Clinical Psychology, 48 (5); 635-9.

Foster, R. (1985). *Money, sex and power.* Hodder and Stoughton, London.

Freud, S. (1962 orig.1930). *Civilization and its Discontents* (trans. J.Strachey). New York; W.W. Norton.

Gillespie, J. (2013). *Beholding Jesus: letters to my children.* Myrrh Books, Overland Park, Kansas.

Harrison, G. (2017). *A Better Story.* Inter-Varsity Press, Cambridge.

Holmes, J. (2001). *Narcissism.* Icon Books, Cambridge.

Jamison, C. (2008). *Finding Happiness: monastic steps for a fulfilling life.* Phoenix, London.

Jernigan, J. (2015). *Redeeming pleasure: how the pursuit of pleasure mirrors our hunger for God.* Worthy, Franklin TN.

Keller, T. (2008). *The Prodigal God.* Riverhead Books, New York.

Kirwan, M (2004). *Discovering Girard.* Barton, Longman and Todd, London.

Koenig, H.G; George, L.K; Peterson, B.L. (1998). *Religiosity and remission of depression in medically ill older patients.* American Journal of Psychiatry, 155, 536-542.

Koenig, H.G; McCullough, M; Larson, D.B. (2012). *Handbook of Religion and Health* (second edition). Oxford University Press, New York.

Kendler, K et al. (2003). Dimensions of religiosity and their relationship to psychiatric and substance misuse disorders. American Journal of Psychiatry, 160; 496-503.

Lewis, C.S. (1996). *The Weight of Glory and Other Addresses.* Ed. W Hopper, Simon and Shuster, New York. (orig.1949. *The Weight of Glory*. The MacMillan Company, New York.)

Lewis, C.S. (1940). *The Problem of Pain.* Centenary Press, London.

Lewis, C.S. (1970). God in the Dock. Eerdmans, Grand Rapids, Michigan.

Lloyd-Jones, D.M. (1998). *Spiritual Depression: Its Causes and Cure.* Marshall Pickering, London (first published 1965).

Moreira-Almeida, A; Neto, F.L; Koenig, H.G. (2006). *Religiousness and Mental Health: a review.* Brazilian Journal of Psychiatry, 28, 242-250.

Pickett, K., & Wilkinson, R. (2010). *The Spirit Level: Why equality is better for everyone.* Penguin, UK.

Punton, J. (1977). *The Community of Shalom: God's Radical Alternative*: Frontier Youth Trust Review, 6,

Rohr, R. (2021). *The World, the Flesh and the Devil: What Do We Do With Evil?* SPCK.

Southgate, C. (2002). *The Groaning of Creation: God, evolution and the problem of evil.* Westminster/ John Knox Press, London.

Smith, T.B; McCullough, M.E; Poll, J. (2003). *Religiousness and Depression: evidence for a main effect and the moderating influence of stressful life events.* Psychological Bulletin, 129, 614-636.

Tennyson, A. (1891). *In Memoriam.* MacMillan and Co, London and New York.

Thielke, H (1964). *How the World Began.* James Clarke, London.

van der Hart, W. & Waller, R. (2014). *The Guilt Book: a path to grace and freedom.* Inter Varsity Press, Nottingham.

Yancey, P. (1988). *Disappointment with God.* Zondervan, Grand Rapids, Michigan.

Printed in Great Britain
by Amazon

33109827R00088